Department of the Environment

Cost Effective Management of Reclaimed Derelict Sites

Land Capability Consultants

Presented to the Science Library by MSc Environmental Forestry 6/91.

London: Her Majesty's Stationery Office

First published 1989
Second impression 1990
ISBN 0 11 752258 9

Preface

This research was carried out by Land Capability Consultants Ltd. between September 1987 and June 1989. The project team comprised:

Keith Jones (Project Director)
Pat Corker
David Watson
Gordon Fisher
Christine Cowley (Associate)
Lindsay Higgins (Report Production)

The work was commissioned by the Inner Cities Directorate of the Department of the Environment and we are grateful to the staff of the Directorate for their help throughout the project. We are particularly grateful to the Department's nominated officers Anthea Nicholson and Elena Kallas. We were assisted throughout by a steering committee which included:

Mr. W. Solesbury	D.o.E., Inner Cities Directorate
Mr. J. Hale	D.o.E., Inner Cities Directorate
Mr. J. Hollingworth	D.o.E., Inner Cities Directorate
Miss A. Ward	D.o.E., Minerals Planning Division
Dr. T. Simpson	D.o.E., Minerals Planning Division
Mr. I. Jamieson	D.o.E., North West Regional Office
Dr. G. Doubleday	Durham County Council
Mr. T. Peace	Durham County Council
Mr. G. Farnell	Kirklees Metropolitan Borough Council
Dr. J. Hopkins	Nature Conservancy Council
Dr. A. Moffatt	Forestry Commission
Mr. M. P. Samuel	Ministry of Agriculture, Fisheries and Food

The Department's Regional Offices provided valuable assistance during the early stages of the project. Local authorities provided the bulk of the information upon which the work was based and without their assistance the research would not have been possible.

We are grateful to all the individuals and organisations who have assisted us during the course of this project.

Contents

List of Tables

List of Figures

List of Plates

Abstract

Research carried out for the Department of the Environment investigating the cost effectiveness of management of sites reclaimed to "soft" end uses under the Derelict Land Grant Scheme is described. The end uses considered comprised public open space, agriculture, recreation, woodland, nature conservation and mixed sites containing two or more of these uses.

The main objectives of the research were to:

i) identify cost effective strategies for the management of reclaimed derelict sites;

ii) assess the extent to which those management strategies are affected by the methods and costs of the initial reclamation.

In order to achieve these objectives details of a representative sample of projects completed between 1978 and 1984 were obtained. The information included details of the pre-reclamation condition of the sites, site investigations and reclamation carried out, and subsequent management of sites with costs where appropriate. The present use and performance of sites was assessed on site visits using a system developed during the project. The information and data obtained are set out in detail in the report.

The information on maintenance operations and costs obtained from local authorities and a range of published and other sources were used to derive "model" operations and costs for maintaining sites. These "models" were based on the main ground cover components present on sites; agricultural grassland, amenity grassland, and trees and shrubs.

The cost effectiveness of schemes was assessed by comparing the capital costs with the performance of sites, maintenance costs with performance and capital costs with maintenance costs. Variation between the cost effectiveness of the various afteruses was evident when assessed in these terms.

The report concludes with discussion of the annual management operations and costs necessary for continued satisfactory performance of sites, cost effective land management strategies for the various types of afteruse considered and the relationship between the capital and maintenance costs and performance of sites. The report includes a summary with recommendations intended to improve the cost effectiveness management of reclaimed derelict sites.

1. Introduction

Management of land restored to 'soft' end uses such as public open space, woodland or recreation is essential. Maintenance requirements are normally greatest in the early years immediately following restoration as vegetation is being established but management at a level appropriate to the use of the land is required in perpetuity. The capital costs of reclamation of derelict land will normally be eligible for government grant aid. However the long term costs of management must be met by the land owner. In the case of sites restored to soft afteruses, this is normally a local authority.

Sources of government funding for land reclamation have been summarised by Burt and Bradshaw (1986). Derelict Land Grant (DLG) is available for those sites falling within the definition of 'derelict', i.e. land so damaged by industrial or other development that it is incapable of beneficial use without treatment. In addition to the direct costs of reclamation the costs of management to ensure successful establishment of vegetation for up to five years after planting is eligible for grant. Current government priorities regarding derelict land reclamation are set out in Department of the Environment Circular 28/85 (DOE 1985). The circular emphasizes the contribution that land reclamation can make to urban renewal and to the supply of building land in urban areas. The essence of government policy is that reclamation should bring about the re-use of land and its disposal, wherever possible for subsequent development. Since 1981 priority has been given to schemes leading to private sector commercial, industrial or residential end uses. In allocating DLG within each region, priority is given to schemes designed to reclaim urban land for such 'hard' private sector end uses.

However the government recognises that where dereliction is extensive, reclamation to achieve environmental improvement is essential in order to attract investors and provide an attractive setting for development. Policy requires that such environmental improvements should be achieved at the minimum necessary cost.

A recent study has evaluated DLG schemes completed between April 1982 and September 1985 (Roger Tym and Partners and Land Use Consultants 1987). Of 931 DLG-aided schemes completed in this period, 36% were restored to 'hard' uses and 64% to 'soft' uses. Because of the policy emphasis on 'hard' end uses, the study placed greatest emphasis on sites intended for such uses. However 52% of the sites studied were returned to 'soft' end uses. The consultants concluded that the environmental benefit of such schemes was high although the full potential of sites was not always realised for various reasons. They suggested that local authorities were not making full use of the grant aid available to cover establishment of vegetation and were committed to high long-term maintenance burdens through specification of seed mixes and tree planting schemes requiring higher levels of maintenance than necessary. They found that too little information on management costs was available to be analysed in detail. The local authorities contacted were concerned about the financial burdens of maintaining sites but were generally not able to identify costs on a site by site basis.

In order that the efficiency of management of derelict sites restored to soft end uses be maximised, it is essential that the costs and effectiveness of management are understood, and the lack of such knowledge is currently limiting the extent to which efficiency of management of restored land can be maximised. This report describes research carried out for the Department of the Environment investigating the cost effectiveness of management of sites reclaimed under the Derelict Land Grant Scheme.

1.1 Objectives and Methods

The main objectives of this research were to:

(i) identify cost effective strategies for the management of reclaimed derelict sites; and

(ii) assess the extent to which those management strategies are affected by the methods and costs of the initial reclamation.

In order to achieve these objectives a sample of projects funded under DLG and completed between 1978 and 1984 was examined. Information on these schemes was obtained from documentary sources comprising Department of the Environment and local authority files, by interviews with the local authority departments responsible for the restoration and management of the sites and by site visits to assess present use and performance. The data collected was analysed to provide information on a number of aspects of reclamation schemes. These included:

(i) the level and nature of the initial site investigation, planning and design of the reclamation scheme;

(ii) characterisation of the physical, chemical and plant nutritional problems for the intended after-uses presented by the derelict sites, and the solutions adopted;

(iii) the nature of, and interaction with, adjoining land uses;

(iv) the costs and timescale of the actual reclamation scheme, subdivided into main items, and funding sources;

(v) costs, timescale and nature of any subsequent Department of the Environment grant-aided establishment of the vegetation (i.e. 1–4 years after planting);

(vi) annual maintenance work on the reclaimed sites, including financial provisions, costs, nature of work and its organisation; and extent to which this requirement was anticipated at scheme design stage;

(vii) legal status, liabilities and land tenure of reclaimed sites, and their land management implications;

(viii) present use and performance of reclaimed sites, assessed by developing and using an agreed set of criteria.

Using this information guidance on the following aspects of land reclamation was derived:

(i) the typical range of annual management costs and the operations required for effective performance of reclaimed derelict sites;

(ii) cost-effective land management strategies for the different afteruses; and

(iii) the relationship between capital costs of reclamation and subsequent mangement costs, performance and strategies adopted.

2. Sample Structure and Survey Methods

Information relating to 835 sites restored to 'soft' afteruses where reclamation was physically completed between April 1978 and March 1984 were provided by Department of the Environment regional offices. These are referred to in this report as the 'available' sites. These sites were categorised by afteruse, size and regional distribution.

2.1 Afteruse Categories

The afteruse categories used were:

— Public Open Space (POS)
— Recreation
— Agriculture
— Woodland
— Nature Conservation
— Mixed

Public open space sites included all those sites to which the public had free access for informal recreation. Sites restored to temporary open space use pending future development for housing, commerce or industry, were also examined (Plates 1 and 2).

Recreation sites were those where some more formal sporting or similar activity took place. Most of them consisted of sports pitches (Plate 3).

Agriculture sites were predominantly permanent grassland used for grazing, silage or hay cropping (Plate 5).

Woodland sites were those where the entire site was planted up with trees regardless of the actual use of the site (Plate 4).

Nature conservation sites were those with a specific conservation use such as Local Nature Reserves or County Naturalist's Trust Reserves (Plate 6).

Mixed sites were those where two or more of the above use categories occupied significant areas of the sites.

The number of sites in each catetory and their regional distribution is shown in Table 2.1.

2.2 The Sample of Sites

A sample of 100 sites was selected from the available sites for detailed study. The composition of this sample was intended to be representative of the available sites as a whole while providing sufficient sites within each category for meaningful comparisons to be made. One site was subsequently found to be unsuitable and the data in this report was obtained from the remaining 99 sites.

2.2.1 Afteruse

72% of the available sites were identified as restored to public open space use. Thus a sample reflecting

Table 2.1 **Afteruse and Regional Distribution of Sites**

DOE Region	POS	Agriculture	Recreation	Woodland	Conservation	Mixed	Total Available Sites
Northern	143	6	7	12	2	41	211
North West/Merseyside	253	10	18	20	–	28	329
Yorks. & Humberside	89	9	4	1	1	22	126
West Midlands	49	–	5	2	1	–	57
East Midlands	35	13	2	1	–	15	66
Eastern	–	–	–	–	–	–	–
South East	–	–	1	–	–	–	1
South West	29	–	3	2	–	4	38
Greater London	7	–	–	–	–	–	7
	605	38	40	38	4	110	835

PLATE 1 Close mown grass with standard amenity trees are a typical feature of small urban public open space.

PLATE 2 Less formal approach to creation of public open space on a small area using block planting of trees and shrubs.

PLATE 3 Typical recreation site. Former quarry reclaimed as a football pitch.

PLATE 4 Woodland planting on colliery spoil heap.

PLATE 5 Large agricultural site on colliery shale in rural setting.

PLATE 6 Magnesian Limestone quarry restored to Local Nature Reserve.

the actual proportion of each afteruse would have resulted in too few examples of the other afteruses. Table 2.2 shows the sample structure adopted.

Table 2.2 **Afteruse of Sample Sites**

Afteruse	Available Sites	Sample	Sample as % of available sites of this type
POS	605	39	6%
Agriculture	38	11	29%
Recreation	40	11	28%
Woodland	38	9	24%
Nature Conservation	4	4	100%
Mixed	110	26	24%
Total:	835	100	12%

With the exception of public open space and nature conservation sites the sample comprised between 24% and 30% of the available sites. In the case of nature conservation the small number of available sites prevented a larger sample size and all four identified sites were included.

Within the mixed site category the end uses included in the 26 sites were as shown in Table 2.3.

Table 2.3 **Afteruses of Mixed Use Sites**

Afteruse	Sites including afteruse	
	No.	%
POS	16	62
Agriculture	15	58
Recreation	6	23
Woodland	16	62
Nature Conservation	4	15
Other	2	8

Public open space, woodland and agriculture were the three most common afteruses within the mixed end use category.

Public open space sites comprised 39% of the sample. In view of the relatively large sample size and wide size variation in these sites, the sample was sub-divided as shown in Table 2.4.

The sample was designed to reflect the size distribution of available sites but with some over-representation of larger sites to provide a sufficiently large sample for study. The use of discrete size classes was intended to clarify the extent to which economies of scale affected the cost of management.

Table 2.4 **Size Distribution of Sites Intended for Public Open Space**

Area (ha)	% of Available POS Sites	Sample No. of Sites	% of Sample of POS Sites
< 0.5	37	11	28
0.6 – 1.0	14	–	–
1.1 – 2.0	16	10	26
2.1 – 5.0	18	–	–
5.1 – 10.0	8	7	18
10.1 – 50.0	7	5	13
Temporary POS	–	6	15
	–	39	100

For sites intended for afteruses other than public open space the sample reflected the overall range of sizes of the available sites but the more limited number of sites necessitated a less formal sample size structure.

2.2.3 Regional Distribution

The regional distribution of the sample broadly reflected the distribution of the available sites as shown in Table 2.5.

Table 2.5 **Regional Distribution of Sample Sites**

Region	Available Sites	Sample	Sample as % of available sites in region
North West and Merseyside	329	30	9%
Northern	211	28	13%
West Midlands	57	10	18%
East Midlands	66	10	15%
Yorks. and Humberside	126	17	13%
South West	38	5	13%
Eastern	0	0	–
South East	1	0	–
Greater London	7	0	–
	835	100	12%

2.3 Selection Strategy

The strategy for selection of sites for study was similar to that described by Roger Tym and Partners and Land Use Consultants (1987). Within each region the minimum number of local authorities which could provide the required number of sites with agriculture, recreation, woodland, nature conservation and mixed afteruses was identified. The public open space sites were then selected from within the same local authorities. The local authorities from which the sample of sites was drawn is shown in Table 2.6.

2.4 Survey Methods

Information on the schemes in the sample was drawn from documentary sources, interviews and site visits. Standard pro-formas were prepared for all sources of information to ensure that data was collected consistently. The main sources of information were the Department of the Environment regional office files, local authorities responsible for reclamation and management of the selected sites, other persons responsible for management (e.g. tenants, licensees or purchasers of completed sites).

Table 2.6 **Local Authorities included in the Sample**

Region and Local Authority	No. of Sites
North West and Merseyside	
Blackburn B.C.	4
Bolton M.B.C.	3
Burnley B.C.	2
Cumbria C.C.	3
Lancashire C.C.	4
Macclesfield B.C.	3
Oldham M.B.C.	2
Pendle B.C.	3
Vale Royal D.C.	3
Wigan M.B.C.	3
Northern	
Chester-le-Street D.C.	5
Cleveland C.C.	2
Durham C.C.	9
Gateshead M.B.C	4
Newcastle City C.	2
Northumberland C.C.	5
West Midlands	
Cannock Chase D.C.	2
Dudley M.B.C	5
Sandwell M.B.C.	3
East Midlands	
Derbyshire C.C.	5
Derbyshire Dales D.C.	1
North East Derbyshire D.C.	2
Nottinghamshire C.C.	3
Yorkshire and Humberside	
Barnsley M.B.C.	2
Doncaster M.B.C.	3
Humberside C.C.	2
Kirklees M.B.C.	8
Former West Yorkshire M.C.C.	2
South West	
Bristol City C.	2
Teignbridge D.C.	1
Torbay B.C.	2

2.4.1 Department of the Environment Regional Office Files

These files were consulted early in the project after an initial short-list of 150 sites had been drawn up. Information collected consisted of:

(i) basic details of site location, size, etc.;

(ii) former use and condition of site prior to reclamation;

(iii) intended post-reclamation land use;

(iv) details of grant applications and approvals;

(v) breakdown of approved costs.

This information was used in the final selection of sites for study.

2.4.2 Local Authorities

The local authorities from which the sample of sites were drawn were each sent sets of forms requesting information on the reclamation and subsequent management of the sites. They were invited to either complete the forms themselves or to permit our staff to do so by means of interview and/or access to relevant files. The information sought was as follows:

2.4.2.1 Reclamation

(i) further details of location, size, condition prior to reclamation, etc.;

(ii) aims of reclamation scheme;

(iii) land use in vicinity of site;

(iv) details of any site investigations carried out;

(v) information regarding site acquisition;

(vi) details of restoration works, costs, contract method, etc.

2.4.2.2 Management

The sites were divided up into management units based on the ground cover present. Information requested regarding management comprised that relating to the site as a whole and that relating to the individual management units making up the site.

These management units were of the following types:

(i) Agricultural grassland.

(ii) Amenity grassland

(iii) Trees/shrubs

(iv) Other ground cover

(v) Water

Information requested regarding site management included:

(i) details of afteruse of site and the nature of the ground cover present;

(ii) information on numbers of people using the site;

(iii) information on management costs and any income.

Information requested regarding unit management included:

(i) details of vegetation, cropping, use, etc.;

(ii) management arrangements;

(iii) details of maintenance and costs during establishment phase and annual maintenance and costs thereafter;

(iv) yields and/or income for the unit where applicable.

Some sites were managed but not maintained directly by the local authority. These were largely sites restored to agricultural land which were farmed by licensees or tenants. In addition some sites had been sold. In these cases management was discussed with those responsible where possible.

2.4.3 Site Inspections

Each site was visited and its present use and performance assessed using a set of criteria developed and agreed during the early stages of the project. This is described fully in section 7.

2.5 Comparison of Costs

The schemes included in the survey were completed during the period April 1978 to March 1984. In order to compare the costs of schemes it was necessary to adjust all costs to a common base year. The year 1986/87 was chosen since it was anticipated that much of the management cost information obtained would relate to that year. Costs were adjusted on the basis of Gross Domestic Product (Market Prices) Deflator updated on 2nd November 1987. The conversion factors are given in Table 2.7.

Table 2.7 **Cost adjustment based on Gross Domestic Product (Market Prices) Deflator (Updated 2nd November 1987)**

Year	G.D.P. Deflator	Multiplier to correct to 1986/87 Costs
1970–71	19.0	5.26
1971–72	20.8	4.81
1972–73	22.4	4.46
1973–74	24.0	4.16
1974–75	28.7	3.49
1975–76	36.0	2.78
1976–77	40.8	2.45
1977–78	46.4	2.15
1978–79	51.4	1.95
1979–80	60.1	1.67
1980–81	71.2	1.40
1981–82	78.2	1.28
1982–83	83.8	1.19
1983–84	87.7	1.14
1984–85	91.5	1.09
1985–86	97.1	1.03
1986–87	100	1.00

3. Restoration Problems and Solutions

3.1 Types of Dereliction

Information on the type of dereliction (i.e. the previous use of the land which had resulted in its derelict condition) was obtained from Department of the Environment regional office files and from local authorities for each site. The types of derelict land were broadly classified into:

(i) Excavations and pits

(ii) Spoil heaps

(iii) General dereliction

(iv) Other dereliction

These main categories were further sub-divided as shown in Table 3.1. As some sites included more than one type of dereliction the total number of sites recorded is greater than 99.

Some categories of dereliction are represented by a sufficient number of sites to make generalisations regarding associations with particular afteruses possible. Colliery spoil heaps were associated with restoration to agriculture, mixed end uses and woodland. Former housing sites were almost universally restored to public open space. Dry excavations (quarries) were most frequently restored to public open space or mixed end uses. To a considerable extent this reflects the location and size of the derelict sites rather than their intrinsic characteristics.

3.2 Site Investigations

The pre-reclamation site investigation work carried out on the sample sites is detailed in Tables 3.2 and 3.3. This information was obtained from the local authorities. For some sites there was uncertainty as to whether surveys were carried out and where this was the case we have assumed that they were not. The frequency with which the main types of survey were carried out varied considerably. Level and drainage surveys and investigations of statutory undertakings were carried out on a high proportion of sites. Investigations of soil nutrient status, soil physical characteristics, underground structures, stability and ecology were carried out on between 25% and 50% of sites. Investigations of soil contamination and combustibility were carried out on less than 25% of sites.

The nature of pre-reclamation site investigations carried out varied between types of site. In some cases the need for particular types of survey was related to the afteruse of the site (e.g. level surveys, drainage surveys, soil nutrient status and physical characteristics). In other cases the need for a particular type of survey was more closely related to the previous use of the site (e.g. contamination, underground structures, stability and combustibility).

Table 3.2 also shows the extent to which local authorities sought advice and assistance from other organisations in carrying out site investigations. Included in "consultants" are private consultants, analysts, MAFF, Nature Conservancy Council, local naturalists' trusts, etc. Such assistance was most commonly sought where surveys included analytical work (e.g. contamination surveys and soil nutrient status) and/or specialist facilities and expertise (e.g. investigation of underground structures and stability) reflecting the normal lack of these specialist skills or facilities within local authorities.

3.3 Physical, Chemical and Plant Nutritional Problems

Specific information regarding the characteristics of sites prior to reclamation was not available to the majority of cases. There were exceptions where individuals with direct knowledge of the schemes were still employed with the local authorities and were able to provide information. The information obtained is discussed here in the context of the general problems associated with derelict sites. Table 3.4 gives an indication of the extent to which site characteristics are of concern in the context of the various afteruses. The afteruses range from those least demanding of site conditions such as nature conservation and public open space, to those most demanding such as agriculture and recreation.

Table 3.1 **Types of Dereliction**

		Public Open Space (POS)					No of Sites						
		<0.5ha	1–2ha	5-10ha	>10ha	Temp.	POS Total	Agric.	Nat. Con.	Wood.	Rec.	Mixed	Total
	Total:	10	11	7	5	6	39	11	4	9	10	26	99
EXCAVATION/ PIT	Wet	0	0	0	0	0	0	0	0	0	0	1	1
	Dry	1	1	0	3	0	5	1	1	0	1	5	13
	Total	1	1	0	3	0	5	1	1	0	1	6	14
SPOIL HEAP	Colliery	0	1	1	2	0	4	6	1	4	1	12	28
	Metalliferous	0	0	0	0	0	0	0	0	0	0	0	0
	Other	0	0	0	1	0	1	0	0	0	1	0	2
	Total	0	1	1	3	0	5	6	1	4	2	12	30
GENERAL DERELICTION	Railway Land	2	2	0	1	0	5	0	0	1	1	3	10
	Canal Land	0	1	0	0	0	1	0	0	0	1	1	3
	Military Land	0	0	0	0	0	0	0	1	0	0	0	1
	Industrial Site	0	3	3	1	2	9	1	1	3	3	8	25
	Industrial Waste Tip	0	0	0	0	1	1	1	0	2	1	3	8
	Household Waste Tip	0	1	1	1	0	3	1	1	0	2	1	8
	Other Waste Tip	0	2	1	0	0	3	2	0	0	0	1	6
	Total	2	9	5	3	3	22	5	3	6	8	17	61
OTHER	Housing Land	4	1	0	0	3	8	0	0	1	0	0	9
	Buildings	2	1	0	0	0	3	0	0	0	0	0	3
	Vacant Land	1	0	1	0	1	3	0	0	1	2	1	7
	Reservoir	0	1	1	0	0	2	1	0	0	1	1	5
	Subsidence	0	0	0	0	0	0	1	1	0	0	2	4
	Sewage Works	0	0	0	0	0	0	1	0	0	0	1	2
	Allotments	1	0	1	0	0	2	0	0	0	0	1	3
	Total	8	3	4	0	4	18	3	1	2	3	6	33

3.3.1 Physical Problems

The main physical problems affecting reclamation were those associated with underground structures such as foundations and mine shafts and those associated with the materials on site such as stability, soil texture and structure, and water holding characteristics.

Mine shafts were of concern for any redevelopment of sites because of the considerable hazard they represent of future users of the site (Plate 7). Mine shafts were associated with 43% of the sites containing colliery spoil heaps and 52% of those containing industrial sites (usually former collieries). In most cases these shafts were capped during reclamation, usually as a separate, specialist contract.

Underground obstruction such as foundations were of most concern for agricultural afteruse of sites where they may prevent any deep cultivations or underdrainage of sites during reclamation or hinder subsequent agricultural operations. Such problems were most often associated with sites of former housing, other buildings and industrial sites.

The texture and structure of materials on derelict sites were often unsatisfactory for plant growth. At one extreme was the open, porous, broken waste rock associated with old quarry workings while at the other were the heavy, impermeable clays associated with old brick workings. Even where the texture of the materials present was satisfactory for plant growth, as is often the case with colliery spoil, the lack of organic matter will prevent the development of good soil structure. Although such problems were relevant to any restoration involving establishment of vegetation, they were particularly so for agriculture or recreation.

Problems of stability were particularly associated with spoil heaps. In the absence of vegetation the steep slopes of heaps are vulnerable to erosion by water and wind (Plate 8). Stability was relevant to all afteruses although in the case of nature conservation some unstable, actively eroding areas may be of benefit in providing habitat for early colonising species. Stability problems were dealt with by regrading and/or establishment of vegetation cover.

Table 3.2 **Pre-Reclamation Site Investigations by Afteruse Categories**

	% of sites at which surveys were carried out											
	Public Open Space (POS)					POS Total	Agric.	Nat. Con.	Wood.	Rec.	Mixed	Total
Site Investigations	<0.5ha	1-2ha	5-10ha	>10ha	Temp.							
Level Surveys carried out	40	55	71	80	50	56	100	50	67	80	88	73
% involving Consultants	0	0	0	0	0	0	9	0	0	13	17	8
Drainage Surveys carried out	70	45	57	80	67	62	82	25	67	60	77	67
% involving Consultants	0	0	0	0	0	0	0	0	0	17	5	3
Contamination Surveys carried out	20	18	43	20	17	23	18	0	33	10	27	22
% involving Consultants	0	50	33	100	0	33	50	0	33	0	57	41
Nutrient Surveys carried out	10	18	14	40	17	18	36	25	33	10	58	31
% involving Consultants	0	0	0	100	0	29	25	0	0	0	67	42
Soil Physical Surveys carried out	20	36	43	60	50	38	64	0	33	40	58	44
% involving Consultants	0	0	0	33	0	7	14	0	33	25	27	18
Underground Structure Surveys carried out	10	45	14	20	17	23	36	25	22	40	27	27
% involving Consultants	0	20	100	100	0	33	50	0	0	50	43	37
Stability Surveys carried out	30	27	29	20	17	26	18	0	11	40	31	25
% involving Consultants	0	33	50	100	0	30	50	0	0	25	50	36
Combustibility Surveys carried out	0	9	57	20	17	18	9	0	0	10	15	13
% involving Consultants	0	0	25	0	0	14	100	0	0	0	50	31
Statutory Undertakers Surveys carried out	0	64	29	60	33	51	73	50	33	60	62	56
% involving Consultants	0	14	0	0	0	5	0	0	0	17	13	7
Ecological Surveys carried out	10	9	29	40	17	18	18	100	56	10	42	30
% involving Consultants	0	0	0	50	0	14	0	50	0	100	9	17

Water may be a problem in establishing vegetation on derelict land both if insufficient or excess is present. Good drainage is essential for successful agricultural or recreational use of land. On all but the most porous, free draining materials, restoration of sites with adequate gradients is essential to ensure good drainage. Piped underdrainage will normally be required for productive agricultural and recreational use of restored sites.

Lack of moisture was also a problem particularly where trees were planted on restored sites. Established trees with deep root systems are able to obtain water from deep within the 'soil'. However young trees are vulnerable to drought during the first few years after planting. The results were frequently seen during the survey where trees were planted on spoil heaps. Those planted near the tops of heaps had often failed, while establishment and growth around the lower slopes was much more successful.

3.3.2 Chemical Problems

The main chemical problems associated with restoration of derelict sites were deficiencies of plant nutrients, the presence of toxic chemicals and the problems of high or low pH. The lack of organic matter to provide a nutrient holding capacity also limits the ability of materials to support plant growth.

The presence of toxic chemicals at a site may represent a hazard to health in addition to affecting the growth and survival of vegetation. Four of the sites in the study were identified as contaminated. These were a gas works site restored to public open space, a tip of waste from a former gas works restored to woodland, a lime waste lagoon contaminated with mercury and other chemicals restored to public open space and private land, and former colliery spoil tips which were used for waste tar disposal restored to agriculture. In all cases restoration involved regrading and import of soils to cover the contaminated materials. We suspect that contamination may have been present at other sites but due to lack of information this is uncertain.

Problems of acidity occurred most frequently on colliery spoil heaps. Iron pyrites commonly occurs in the shales associated with coal seams. On exposure to the air this oxidises to sulphuric acid resulting in very low pH values in the surface layers of spoil

Table 3.3 **Pre-Reclamation Site Investigations by Type of Dereliction**

Site Investigations:		Level Survey	Drainage Survey	Contam. Survey	Nutrient Survey	Soil Physical Survey	U'ground Struct. Survey	Stability Survey	Combust. Survey	Statutory U'takers Survey	Ecol. Survey
		% of Sites									
EXCAVATION/ PIT	Wet	100	0	0	100	100	100	0	0	100	0
	Dry	85	77	15	15	38	8	31	15	69	46
	Total	86	71	14	21	43	14	29	14	71	43
SPOIL HEAP	Colliery	86	64	36	61	57	39	32	25	64	36
	Metalliferous	0	0	0	0	0	0	0	0	0	0
	Other	100	100	0	0	50	0	0	0	100	0
	Total	87	67	33	57	57	37	30	23	67	33
GENERAL DERELICTION	Railway Land	80	50	10	30	40	10	20	0	50	50
	Canal Land	33	67	0	33	33	33	0	0	33	0
	Military Land	0	0	0	0	0	100	0	0	0	100
	Industrial Site	76	80	40	52	52	40	36	28	68	36
	Industrial Waste Tip	100	75	50	50	88	25	13	0	38	50
	Household Waste Tip	88	25	0	13	38	13	25	0	38	50
	Other Waste Tip	50	50	17	0	33	0	33	0	67	0
	Total	75	62	26	36	49	26	26	11	54	38
OTHER	Housing Land	11	56	0	0	22	11	0	0	44	0
	Buildings	33	33	33	0	0	33	67	0	67	0
	Vacant Land	57	71	14	0	29	14	14	0	43	14
	Reservoir	100	80	20	0	20	80	40	20	60	20
	Subsidence	50	50	0	0	25	0	0	0	25	25
	Sewage Works	100	100	0	50	50	0	0	0	50	0
	Allotments	100	100	0	0	0	0	0	0	33	0
	Total	55	67	9	3	21	21	15	3	45	9

Table 3.4 **General Extent to which Site Characteristics present Problems for Afteruse of Sites.**

Characteristic	Nat. Con.	POS	Afteruse Wood	Agr.	Rec.
Mine shafts	***	***	***	***	***
Underground obstructions	*	*	**	***	**
Soil texture + structure	*	**	**	***	***
Stability	**	***	***	***	***
Moisture	**	**	***	***	***
Nutrient status	*	*	*	**	**
pH	**	**	**	***	***
Toxicity	**	**	**	***	***

* Low concern
** Some concern
*** Major concern

heaps. The problems were dealt with either by covering the spoil with soil during restoration or by heavy applications of lime to neutralise the acidity. Such applications must be sufficient to cope with weathering of residual unoxidised pyrite in the spoil or regression of vegetation will occur. Such problems were evident on some sites. At two sites lime treatment was not successful and the extent of regression was such that initial reclamation was considered to have failed (Plate 9).

Highly alkaline materials can also present problems for vegetation establishment largely through immobilisation of phosphate and micronutrients. Examples of high pH materials encountered in the survey were waste tips from lime burning and waste lime beds from the production of sodium carbonate. Restoration of these sites involved covering with imported soils. Some old lime waste deposits have developed an interesting flora naturally after a prolonged period of weathering. The high pH and low nutrient status are an advantage under the circumstances.

3.4 Reclamation Techniques Adopted

The treatments used in reclamation of the sites studied ranged from minimal treatments utilising vegetation cover which had naturally colonised the site to major earthmoving and regrading, importing

PLATE 7
Open mine shaft on reclaimed derelict site. Such shafts were common on former colliery sites and spoil heaps but were normally capped during reclamation.

PLATE 8
Gully erosion of colliery spoil due to compaction, steep slope and lack of vegetation.

PLATE 9 Oxidation of iron pyrites in colliery spoil produces acid soil conditions which may be neutralised with lime. This site received lime treatment at reclamation but subsequent oxidation of iron pyrites in combination with consolidation and lack of structure has resulted in death of vegetation.

PLATE 10 Vertical section through restored soil profile showing topsoil cover over colliery spoil reclaimed for agricultural use.

of soils and establishment of vegetation in this newly placed material. The types of treatment adopted were classified into four types as shown in Table 3.5. Since some sites included areas where different treatments were used the number of sites included in the table is greater than 100%.

The extent to which the various treatments were used depended to a considerable extent on the afteruse of sites although the types of dereliction also influenced the types of treatment used.

Minimal treatment was commonly adopted at sites including dry excavations. These included sandstone and limestone quarries. Major regrading and import of soils was particularly associated with colliery spoil heaps and industrial sites and waste tips (Plate 10). Import of topsoil without other major earthworks was frequent at sites of former housing and other buildings, reservoirs and allotments, railway land and household waste tips.

3.4.1 Planning and Design of Reclamation Schemes

The planning and design of reclamation schemes was carried out almost exclusively by local authority staff. The only exception was a nature conservation site where the overall concept and outline scheme was prepared by a private landscape architect.

Information on the organisation of reclamation planning and design was obtained from seventeen local authorities. Initiation of schemes in most cases was by planning departments. In one local authority an interdepartmental derelict land working group recommended schemes to the planning department. In one county council schemes were initiated by a department of economic development.

The extent of early work on schemes prior to council committee approval varied considerably between local authorities. Seven of the authorities (41%) had reclamation working parties or similar interdepartmental groups who met on a regular basis to progress schemes. In some cases these were attended by Department of the Environment regional office representatives. In four (24%) of the authorities little work was done prior to committee approval because of limited resources. Estates and valuers departments were often involved in early discussions particularly where land acquisition was necessary.

The detailed design of 'soft' end use schemes was carried out by one of three types of department, either Planning/Development Services (53%), Engineering/Technical Services (35%) or Leisure Services/Parks Dept. (12%). In most cases the lead department involved other departments in detailed design where necessary.

Fifteen (88%) of the authorities stated that they considered the long term management costs of schemes as part of the design process. In one of the remaining authorities costs for a five year establishment plan were considered.

3.5 Relationship with Adjoining Land Uses

The nature of the locations of each of the sites was classified according to the nature of the surrounding land uses and their influence on the sites. The classification used was:

Urban – Entirely surrounded by land uses of an urban nature such as housing, industry or commerce.

Urban Fringe – On the edge of large urban centres or adjacent to smaller settlements and influenced by their presence.

Rural – Rural locations not directly influenced by settlements.

Table 3.6 shows the sites within each of the afteruse categories classified in this way. Public open space sites smaller than 0.5 ha were all in urban locations. The majority of those in the 1-2 ha size class were

Table 3.5 **Reclamation Techniques by Afteruse**

		Public Open Space (POS)					POS	Agric.	Nat.	Wood.	Rec.	Mixed	Total
		<0.5ha	1-2ha	5-10ha	>10ha	Temp.	Total		Con.				
MINIMAL TREATMENT	No. of Sites	1	2	1	2	0	6	1	4	1	1	7	20
	% of Sites	10	18	14	40	0	15	9	100	11	10	27	20
EXISTING SOIL	No. of Sites	1	4	0	1	1	7	3	2	6	2	3	23
	% of Sites	10	36	0	20	17	18	27	50	67	20	12	23
IMPORT TOPSOIL	No. of Sites	4	8	3	2	2	19	2	0	1	7	10	39
	% of Sites	40	73	43	40	33	49	18	0	11	70	38	39
MAJOR REGRADING ETC.	No. of Sites	4	1	3	1	3	12	8	1	4	5	16	46
	% of Sites	40	9	43	20	50	31	73	25	44	50	62	46

urban while for sites above 5 ha in size urban fringe locations increase in importance. Temporary public open space and recreation sites were also predominantly urban in location.

Agriculture, nature conservation and woodland afteruses were predominantly in rural locations while mixed afteruses were most common in urban fringe settings.

Table 3.6 **Location of Sites**

	No. of Sites	% of Sites		
		Urban	Urban Fringe	Rural
POS <0.5 ha	10	100	0	0
POS 1-2 ha	11	55	27	18
POS 5-10 ha	7	29	57	14
POS >10 ha	5	40	40	20
POS Temporary	6	83	17	0
Agriculture	11	0	36	64
Woodland	9	22	22	56
Nature Conservation	4	0	25	75
Recreation	10	70	30	0
Mixed	26	12	54	34

3.5.1 Types of Adjacent Land Use

Information on land uses adjoining reclaimed sites was provided by local authorities and confirmed on site visits. The land uses were classified as shown in Table 3.7. The land uses most commonly adjoining reclaimed sites were housing, agriculture and amenity. Almost all the public open space sites and most of the recreation sites were adjacent to housing. Agricultural land adjoining all the sites which were restored to agriculture and most of those restored to woodland. Of those sites restored to public open space, only the larger sites tended to be adjacent to agricultural land.

Land with an amenity use was relatively common adjacent to reclaimed land of most types particularly large public open space sites. Forestry and commerce were rarely encountered adjoining reclaimed sites.

Land uses within the 'other' category included major roads, school, hospitals, etc.

3.5.2 Interaction with Adjacent Land Uses

Evidence of interactions between reclaimed sites and their surroundings was sought during site visits. The degree to which afteruse of the sites depended on their surroundings varied considerably. The category of site where use was most closely related to that of the surrounding land was agriculture. Sites were invariably occupied by farmers of adjacent or nearby holdings as owners, tenants or licensees. Use of the sites for agriculture depends on the continued existence of other agricultural land in the vicinity.

The category of site where use was least closely related to surrounding land uses was woodland. In most cases these were isolated blocks of planting with no strong management relationship with other land in the vicinity, although frequently of potentially high visual importance in the landscape.

The positive effects of the sites on their surroundings as measured in terms of amenity use and landscape value are discussed in section 6.1 of this report.

The extent to which sites were affected by their surroundings were also assessed during site visits. The degree of public pressure at each site was assessed in terms of the type and density of housing nearest to the site, the accessibility of the site from housing, the presence and accessibility of the site to schools and use of the site as a through route. As described in section 6.0 a score out of 20 was calculated for each site. The average scores for each afteruse are shown in Table 3.8. The higher the score shown in the table, the greater the degree of public pressure to which the sites were subjected. Although there is considerable overlap between scores for individual size classes, the high degree of pressure on small public open space sites is evident as is a decrease with increasing size of site.

The degree of public pressure was least for agriculture and nature conservation sites which tended to be in relatively remote locations. Woodland, recreation and mixed sites were intermediate in terms of public pressure.

In addition to overall assessment of public pressure at the sites a number of indicators of adverse effects were recorded as shown in Table 3.9. The categories of afteruse may be ranked in terms of the occurrence of the main types of adverse effect recorded. The average ranking for each afteruse is shown in the table. It can be seen that the occurrence of adverse effects on sites is closely correlated with the degree of public pressure for the afteruse categories shown in Table 3.8. Public open space sites suffered most adverse effects while agriculture and nature conservation sites were little affected. Woodland, recreation and mixed sites were intermediate.

3.6 Land Tenure

Information on land ownership was obtained from Department of the Environment regional offices and local authorities.

Table 3.7 **Land Uses adjacent to Reclaimed Sites**

		Public Open Space (POS)					POS	Agric.	Nat.	Wood.	Rec.	Mixed	Total
		<0.5ha	1-2ha	5-10ha	>10ha	Temp.	Total		Con.				
	Total:	10	11	7	5	6	39	11	4	9	10	26	99
AGRICULTURE	No. of Sites	0	4	5	3	1	13	11	2	8	2	21	57
	% of Sites	0	36	71	60	17	33	100	50	89	20	81	58
FORESTRY	No. of Sites	0	0	0	2	0	2	1	1	0	0	0	4
	% of Sites	0	0	0	40	0	5	9	25	0	0	0	4
AMENITY/ RECREATION	No. of Sites	3	7	6	5	2	23	6	1	2	5	16	53
	% of Sites	30	64	86	10	33	59	55	25	22	50	62	54
NATURE CONSERVATION	No. of Sites	0	1	1	1	0	3	3	2	0	2	5	15
	% of Sites	0	9	14	20	0	8	27	50	0	20	19	15
INDUSTRY	No. of Sites	4	5	2	1	4	1	4	0	4	3	12	39
	% of Sites	40	45	29	20	67	41	36	0	44	30	46	39
COMMERCE	No. of Sites	2	0	0	0	1	3	0	0	0	0	1	4
	% of Sites	20	0	0	0	17	8	0	0	0	0	4	4
HOUSING	No. of Sites	9	10	6	4	4	33	4	1	4	8	17	67
	% of Sites	90	91	86	80	67	85	36	25	44	80	65	68
UNUSED	No. of Sites	0	2	1	1	2	6	2	0	2	1	8	19
	% of Sites	0	18	14	20	33	15	18	0	22	10	31	19
OTHER	No. of Sites	6	5	3	3	4	21	2	2	5	5	12	47
	% of Sites	60	45	43	60	67	54	18	50	56	50	46	47

Table 3.8 **Public Pressure Assessment**

	Public Open Space (POS)					Agric.	Nat.	Wood	Rec.	Mixed
	<0.5ha	1-2ha	5-10ha	>10ha	Temp		Con.			
MEAN SCORE	11.0	9.7	8.9	7.7	9.8	4.6	5.2	6.1	8.5	7.5
S.D.	3.4	3.3	4.3	3.8	3.1	2.6	2.2	3.5	3.2	3.2

3.6.1. Pre-Reclamation Ownership

Table 3.10 gives information regarding local authority ownership of sites before reclamation. Approximately half the sites were already in local authority ownership prior to their reclamation. All but two of the remaining sites were purchased or leased with the aid of DLG in order that they could be restored.

The local authorities' powers of compulsory purchase were used in order to acquire land in connection with seven of the reclamation schemes.

3.6.2 Post-Reclamation Land Ownership

Table 3.11 shows information concerning the current ownership and tenure of the sites included in the survey. Almost all the sites included areas which remain in local authority ownership. The exceptions were one public open space site owned by a water authority, a nature conservation site owned by a local naturalist's trust, a mixed end use site leased from an industrial company and four agricultural sites sold to farming concerns. Local authorities are directly involved in management of 87% of the sites. All the public open space sites are directly managed by local authorities as are all the woodland sites. Local authorities also manage at least some part of all the sites restored to mixed end uses.

Local authorities did not maintain any agricultural land directly. Of the seven agricultural sites retained in local authority ownership, six were let on annual grazing licences and one was tenanted. Of the areas of agricultural land in mixed end use sites, two had been sold and ten were let on annual grazing licence, two were tenanted and one was let on a long term lease. Two of the mixed end use sites included allotments which were tenanted.

One of the recreation sites was leased to a charitable trust and two of the three nature conservation sites in local authority ownership included areas managed under licence by nature conservation trusts.

Table 3.9 **Adverse Effects of Site Use**

		Public Open Space (POS) <0.5ha	1-2ha	5-10ha	>10ha	Temp.	Agric.	Nat. Con.	Wood.	Rec.	Mixed
	Total:	10	11	7	5	6	11	4	9	10	26
VEGETATION DAMAGE	No. of Sites	8	7	4	5	5	4	2	5	6	15
	% of Sites	80	64	57	100	83	36	50	56	60	58
	Rank	8	7	4	10	9	1	2	3	6	5
LITTER	No. of Sites	7	7	5	4	6	2	2	5	7	15
	% of Sites	70	64	71	80	100	18	50	56	70	58
	Rank	6	5	8	9	10	1	2	3	6	4
GARDEN DUMPING	No. of Sites	3	4	3	2	2	1	1	1	2	7
	% of Sites	30	36	43	40	33	9	25	11	20	27
	Rank	6	8	10	9	7	1	4	2	3	5
GFENERAL DUMPING	No. of Sites	4	6	2	2	2	2	0	5	3	8
	% of Sites	40	55	29	40	33	18	0	56	30	31
	Rank	7	9	3	7	6	2	1	10	4	5
VANDALISM	No. of Sites	9	4	4	2		4	1	5	7	17
	% of Sites	90	36	57	40	0	36	25	56	70	65
	Rank	10	2	7	4	5	2	1	6	9	8
MEAN RANK		7	6	6	8	7	1	2	5	6	5

Table 3.10 **Pre-Reclamation Land Ownership**

		Public Open Space (POS) <0.5ha	1-2ha	5-10ha	>10ha	Temp.	POS Total	Agric.	Nat. Con.	Wood.	Rec.	Mixed	Total
	Total:	10	1	7	5	6	39	11	4	9	10	26	99
SITE OWNED BY L.A.	No. of Sites	9	6	3	3	4	25	3	1	4	5	7	45
	% of Sites	90	55	43	60	67	64	27	25	44	50	27	45
PURCHASED WITH DLG	No. of Sites	1	4	4	2	2	13	8	3	5	5	18	52
	% of Sites	10	36	57	40	33	33	73	75	56	50	69	53
COMPULSORY PURCHASE	No. of Sites	0	0	0	0	0	0	0	1	1	1	4	7
	% of Sites	0	0	0	0	0	0	0	25	11	10	15	7

Table 3.11 **Post-Reclamation Land Ownership**

		Public Open Space (POS) <0.5ha	1-2ha	5-10ha	>10ha	Temp.	POS Total	Agric.	Nat. Con.	Wood.	Rec.	Mixed
SITES OWNED AND MANAGED BY L.A.	No. of Sites	10	11	7	4	6	38	7	3	9	10	25
	% of Sites	100	100	100	80	100	97	64	75	100	100	96
SITES SOLD	No. of Sites	0	0	0	0	0	0	4	0	0	0	2
	% of Sites	0	0	0	0	0	0	36	0	0	0	8
OTHER SITES NOT IN L.A. OWNERSHIP	No. of Sites	0	0	0	1	0	1	0	1	0	0	1
	% of Sites	0	0	0	20	0	3	0	25	0	0	4
SITES MAINTAINED BY L.A.	No. of Sites	10	11	7	5	6	39	0	3	9	9	26
	% of Sites	100	100	100	100	100	100	0	75	100	90	100
SITES LICENSED	No. of Sites	0	0	0	0	0	0	6	2	0	0	10
	% of Sites	0	0	0	0	0	0	55	50	0	0	38
SITES TENANTED	No of Sites	0	0	0	0	0	0	1	0	0	0	2
	% of Sites	0	0	0	0	0	0	9	0	0	0	8
SITES LEASED	No. of Sites	0	0	0	0	0	0	0	0	0	1	1
	% of Sites	0	0	0	0	0	0	0	0	0	10	4

Note: 1. Some nature conservation sites jointly maintained by L.A./Local Naturalists' Trust.
2. Agricultural component of mixed sites not directly maintained by L.A.

It can be seen that agriculture was the main afteruse where land was not normally maintained directly by local authorities. Although some authorities had sold land restored to agriculture, there was generally a preference to retain such land in order that some degree of control over its management was retained. The main types of agreements under which agricultural land may be occupied include:

3.6.2.1 '364 day' grazing/mowing licences This is a licence for occupation of the land for grazing or mowing for less than one year. A period of 364 days is often specified and there may be a requirement to remove stock from the land on the 365th day to ensure that a full tenancy is not established. It is important that the occupier does not perform operations such as fertilizing, ploughing or repairing hedges since he may claim that a full tenancy, with its attendant rights of tenure, has been established.

3.6.2.2 Short term lettings and licences Sections 2 and 5 of the 1986 Agricultural Holdings Act provide for short term lettings or licences approved by the Ministry of Agriculture, Fisheries and Food. Lettings of less than one year or licences for more than one year may be approved. If a landlord and prospective tenant apply jointly in writing a letting for not less than two or no more than five years may be approved. Approval for such lettings will only be given where it is unreasonable to expect a landlord to let the land on a full tenancy. This may be the case where development of land is pending; where temporary arrangements for cultivation must be made as for example when land is to be sold or re-let; where a landlord wishes to give a new tenant a trial period or where a farmer wishes to let land to a specialist grower for a crop not normally grown on the holding.

3.6.2.3 'Gladstone v. Bower' tenancies These are tenancies for terms of more than one year but less than two years which do not fall within either Section 2 or Section 3 of the 1986 Act. The legal standing of these tenancies is uncertain and although not attracting security of tenure they may enable tenants to claim compensation for improvements.

3.6.2.4 Agricultural tenancies This is the normal system of land tenure in this country. The landlord provides and maintains the land and infrastructure required to farm it such as buildings, roads etc. The tenant provides the livestock, machinery and materials such as fertilizers, seed etc, needed. The tenant pays an annual rent to the landlord. The rights and obligations of landlord and tenant are governed by the Agricultural Holdings Act 1986. In particular the tenant has security of tenure and there is a right of succession.

3.6.2.5 *Tenure considerations* Some authorities were concerned that regression of restored land could occur and that this would cause difficulties if the land was no longer in their ownership. This desire to retain control of the land was also reflected in the method of letting which was most widely used i.e. short term grazing or mowing licences. The extent to which licensees carry out maintenance operations on the restored sites, other than simply grazing and mowing, varied. In many cases the licensees undertook complete management of the land. In other cases licensees were advised by the local authority and applied fertilizers supplied by the local authority. In general the licensees undertook a greater proportion of the management of the land than would normally be expected under a short term licence.

As discussed in section 8.2.2, management of derelict land reclaimed to agriculture should aim to maintain the land in an acceptable physical and visual condition while minimising local authorities' maintenance costs. In order to achieve these aims and protect their interests as landowners, it is essential that authorities obtain the highest standard of estate management advice. It is beyond the scope of this study to discuss other than in very general terms the various management options and the most appropriate strategies will vary between sites.

In considering management arrangements a number of aspects must be given careful consideration. Tenure arrangements have effects on the freehold value of the land. Land with vacant possession has a higher value than tenanted land. The actual vacant possession premium varies from year to year but can exceed 50% The implications of the Occupiers Liability Act of 1957 and 1984 must be considered. The economic aspects of the various tenure options including income and expenditure predictions for the occupier and landowner together with taxation, rating and V.A.T. implications must be taken into account.

It is essential that the selection of tenants and licensees is made with care and the use of short term lettings for trial periods may be advantageous.

4. Reclamation Costs

Information on the costs of reclamation work was obtained initially from Department of the Environment project files. More detailed costs were obtained from local authorities where information was available. In all cases costs were converted to 1986/87 prices as described in section 2.5. Figures quoted throughout this chapter are mean 1986/87 costs per hectare ± one standard deviation. Tables 4.1 to 4.9 and 4.13 show the costs of reclamation operations for the various afteruses of sites. In these tables the number of sites in which the particular costs were incurred is indicated and this figure is also expressed as a percentage of the number of sites for which information was available. As would be expected these costs were in general highly variable and site specific. This high variability means that few statistically significant differences between means of costs of reclamation work could be identified between the various afteruse categories. However trends are evident in the data and it is these trends which are discussed in this section.

Information on the time taken for the main items of reclamation work carried out was sought but the information was not available for the majority of sites. The extent of the available information does not permit any detailed assessment of these timescales.

4.1 Acquisition Costs

Information on costs of acquiring land for reclamation was based largely on information from Department of the Environment files. These costs varied widely. The overall average acquisition cost for the 54 sites where land was purchased was £5,740 ± 17,200. However this includes four sites with very high costs of £14,200, £24,600, £88,000 and £92,600 per ha. If these are excluded the average cost of acquisition of the remaining 50 sites is £1,810 ± 1,610. This represents a more realistic average cost of land acquisition. The costs for these 50 sites range from £20 to £7,594 per ha. Where no acquisition costs were incurred land was normally in local authority ownership prior to reclamation (see Section 3.6).

4.2 Site Clearance

This included the cost of any demolition work and removal of foundations or other unwanted materials prior to reclamation. Tables 4.1 and 4.2 show the costs for the various afteruses. Demolition work of some kind was carried out on a high proportion of the schemes. The costs were highly variable and site specific and average costs were not very meaningful. However it can be seen that the highest costs were associated with small public open space sites which were typically urban and included former housing or other buildings (Plate 11).
Off site disposal of material occurred in a much lower proportion of schemes and high costs were again associated with small public open space sites.

4.3 Engineering Works

This included regrading of sites, import and placement of fill and subsoil and drainage. Costs of regrading are shown in Table 4.3. Regrading was carried out on the majority of sites as discussed in section 3.3. With the exception of the high costs associated with public open space sites of less than 0.5 ha and temporary open space sites, the average costs for regrading were in the range £2,000 – £5,000 per hectare.

Import of material other than topsoil occurred in nine (9%) of the schemes included in the survey. The costs varied widely between £37 and £17,500/ha. It should be noted that in the case of those sites with very low costs not all the area was treated.

Costs of drainage are shown in Table 4.4. Drainage works were carried out on a high proportion of the sites. In particular all the agricultural schemes where

Table 4.1 **Cost of Demolition £/ha**

	No. of Sites	% of Sites	Mean	Range
POS <0.5 ha	8	100	7600	375 – 36400
POS 1–2 ha	8	89	3580	32 – 15500
POS 5–10 ha	6	100	415	99 – 880
POS >10 ha	4	80	432	54 – 935
POS Temporary	2	67	373	358 – 388
Agriculture	9	100	762	75 – 1980
Woodland	7	88	2720	234 – 7200
Nature Conservation	2	67	113	46 – 180
Recreation	8	89	2620	42 – 7130
Mixed	17	65	649	15 – 2903

PLATE 11 Reclamation of urban sites frequently incurs high clearance costs as a result of small size and restricted access.

PLATE 12 The potential afteruse of many small urban sites is restricted by their size and location. Schemes are often unimaginative and uninteresting.

Table 4.2 **Cost of Disposal of Material £/ha**

	No. of Sites	% of Sites	Mean	Range
POS <0.5 ha	3	38	8310	370 – 23800
POS 1–2 ha	4	44	1700	210 – 3420
POS 5–10 ha	1	17	4000	–
POS >10 ha	2	40	495	54 – 935
POS Temporary	2	67	3830	134 – 7530
Agriculture	4	44	988	380 – 1980
Woodland	1	13	797	–
Nature Conservation	1	33	173	–
Recreation	4	44	2230	42 – 4210
Mixed	4	19	3890	22 – 12000

Table 4.3 **Cost of Regrading £/ha**

	No. of Sites	% of Sites	Mean	Range
POS <0.5 ha	7	88	11100	804 – 48300
POS 1–2 ha	5	56	3220	586 – 7050
POS 5–10 ha	6	100	3980	145 – 17800
POS >10 ha	5	100	4130	145 – 17300
POS Temporary	3	100	9840	4450 – 13400
Agriculture	9	100	3610	357 – 9000
Woodland	7	88	3110	715 – 8370
Nature Conservation	2	66	2090	951 – 3220
Recreation	9	100	4570	515 – 12900
Mixed	20	95	5030	47 – 25200

Table 4.4 **Cost of Drainage £/ha**

	No. of Sites	% of Sites	Mean	Range
POS <0.5 ha	4	50	17700	301 – 46200
POS 1–2 ha	5	56	1870	65 – 7420
POS 5–10 ha	5	83	809	87 – 1240
POS >10 ha	5	100	945	247 – 1610
POS Temporary	2	66	3120	1630 – 4610
Agriculture	6	67	3040	73 – 7790
Woodland	5	63	2030	85 – 6130
Nature Conservation	3	100	840	97 – 1453
Recreation	7	70	4770	264 – 13800
Mixed	16	76	3090	331 – 26100

cost information was available included drainage works. This was also true of the nature conservation sites, perhaps surprisingly. However it can be seen from the costs that these works were not extensive. Within the public open space category, the proportion of sites requiring drainage work increased with increasing size of site, while the highest costs were associated with smaller sites.

With the exception of small public open space sites the highest drainage costs were associated with restoration to recreation reflecting the need for intensive drainage provision for winter pitches.

4.4 Ground Preparation and Planting

These works included the cost of importing and placing topsoil, together with cultivation, seeding and planting (including support and protection of trees and shrubs). The seeding and planting costs normally included the cost of initial establishment work carried out under the landscaping contract, usually one growing season.

The costs of importing topsoil are shown in Table 4.5. None of the woodland schemes demanded import of topsoil. At some sites suitable topsoil for restoration was present on site, but in the majority of cases trees were planted directly into waste materials. Topsoil was not normally used in restoration for nature conservation and public open space sites above 10 ha in size. At those sites where topsoil was used, this was in selected areas and not to cover the whole site. The costs, however, were calculated on the basis of the sites as a whole.

With the exception of the largest public open space sites imported topsoil was used on the majority of sites restored to this afteruse. The costs per hectare decrease with increasing size of site. Topsoil was used for most of those schemes involving restoration to agriculture and recreation.

Table 4.5 **Cost of Importing Topsoil £/ha**

	No. of Sites	% of Sites	Mean	Range
POS <0.5 ha	5	83	7130	5520 – 8500
POS 1–2 ha	6	67	3810	784 – 6230
POS 5–10 ha	5	83	2510	380 – 7200
POS >10 ha	1	20	220	–
POS Temporary	2	66	4340	1520 – 7160
Agriculture	8	89	6580	352 – 18700
Woodland	0	00	–	–
Nature Conservation	1	33	78	–
Recreation	7	78	8750	4170 – 18700
Mixed	8	38	2390	380 – 3930

Table 4.6 **Cost of Cultivations £/ha**

	No. of Sites	% of Sites	Mean	Range
POS <0.5 ha	8	100	2570	800 – 5990
POS 1–2 ha	3	38	2170	331 – 3922
POS 5–10 ha	5	83	567	111 – 1241
POS >10 ha	4	80	1990	44 – 3914
POS Temporary	2	66	1650	1510 – 1790
Agriculture	8	89	1600	337 – 3300
Woodland	7	88	1350	248 – 4390
Nature Conservation	2	66	760	97 – 1420
Recreation	8	89	2180	120 – 9140
Mixed	19	90	668	46 – 1530

Costs of cultivations carried out as part of restoration work are shown in Table 4.6. Average cultivation costs were typically between £1,600 and £2,200 per hectare. Costs for small public open space sites were slightly higher and those for woodland slightly lower. Low costs were associated with restoration to nature conservation and public open space sites between 5 and 10 ha and mixed uses where cultivations were normally carried out on selected areas of sites.

Costs of grass seeding are shown in Table 4.7. Average costs were typically in the range £400 to £1,100/ha. The average cost for recreation sites was slightly higher, possibly reflecting the use of more specialised seed mixtures and higher seeding rates. Costs for nature conservation sites were low as seeding was selective.

Tree planting costs are shown in Table 4.8. Some planting was carried out on all sites with the exception of most temporary and some small public open space sites. The nature of planting varied considerably between afteruse categories. In the case of woodland sites the entire area was normally planted with transplants or whips. Planting on small public open space sites normally consisted of a small number of standard trees in amenity grassland (Plate 12). Between these extremes many sites included blocks of amenity plantings using a mixture of standards and whips. In spite of these various different types of planting, the typical average costs for the various afteruse categories were between £1,000 and £2,000 per hectare.

Unit area costs were high for small public open space sites (Plate 13). Planting on agriculture, nature conservation and mixed sites tended to be in relatively small areas in comparison to the size of the sites and this is reflected in the lower average costs (Plate 14).

Table 4.7 **Cost of Seeding £/ha**

	No. of Sites	% of Sites	Mean	Range
POS <0.5 ha	6	100	1050	231 – 2050
POS 1–2 ha	4	67	874	337 – 2190
POS 5–10 ha	5	100	579	107 – 1890
POS >10 ha	2	66	615	261 – 968
POS Temporary	2	100	4310	1210 – 7400
Agriculture	8	100	604	105 – 1060
Woodland	5	63	403	76 – 1190
Nature Conservation	2	66	103	10 – 196
Recreation	6	100	1490	653 – 3480
Mixed	20	100	351	79 – 1530

Table 4.8 **Cost of Planting £/ha**

	No. of Sites	% of Sites	Mean	Range
POS <0.5 ha	5	83	2780	1570 – 4360
POS 1–2 ha	6	100	2180	107 – 4770
POS 5–10 ha	5	100	1990	555 – 4540
POS >10 ha	3	75	1010	663 – 1510
POS Temporary	1	33	12300	–
Agriculture	7	88	782	132 – 2889
Woodland	8	100	1390	798 – 2040
Nature Conservation	3	100	192	124 – 228
Recreation	6	100	1730	369 – 3960
Mixed	21	100	724	127 – 1640

Table 4.9 Cost of Fencing £/ha

	No. of Sites	% of Sites	Mean	Range
POS <0.5 ha	5	63	9330	1670 – 20000
POS 1–2 ha	5	56	2570	165 – 8740
POS 5–10 ha	4	67	956	45 – 1950
POS >10 ha	5	100	681	11 – 1570
POS Temporary	2	67	2570	666 – 4480
Agriculture	7	78	1610	341 – 3040
Woodland	8	75	1160	43 – 2610
Nature Conservation	3	100	905	328 – 1780
Recreation	7	78	1200	269 – 3500
Mixed	21	90	1200	14 – 7060

Costs of fencing are shown in Table 4.9. Average costs for the various afteruses were typically in the range £900 – £1,600 per hectare. Average costs of fencing small public open space sites with a larger edge:area ratio were much higher, while the converse is true of large public open space sites.

4.5 Overall Costs of Reclamation

Table 4.10 summarises the costs of actual reclamation work for each category of afteruse. In Table 4.11 these costs are weighted according to the percentage of sites within each category at which the operations were carried out.

The effect of size of site on costs of reclamation is clearly seen for the public open space sites. Costs of restoration to temporary public open space are relatively high since these sites tend to be relatively small (average area 1.2 ± 0.7 ha). Restoration to recreation was the most costly of the remaining afteruses. Restoration to nature conservation was the least costly reflecting the high proportion of these sites where existing vegetation was retained.

Table 4.10 **Mean Costs of Reclamation Schemes £/ha**

	Public Open Space <0.5 ha	1–2 ha	5–10 ha	>10 ha	Temporary	Agriculture	Woodland	Nature Conservation	Recreation	Mixed
Demolition	7600	3580	415	432	373	762	2720	113	2620	649
Disposal	8310	1700	4000	495	3830	988	797	173	2230	3890
Regrading	11100	3210	3980	4130	9840	3610	3110	2090	4570	5030
Drainage	17700	1870	809	945	3120	3040	2030	840	4770	3090
Topsoil	7130	3810	2510	220	4340	6580	0	78	8750	2390
Cultivation	2570	2170	567	1990	1650	1600	1350	760	2180	668
Seeding	1050	874	579	615	4310	604	403	103	1490	351
Planting	2780	2180	1990	1010	12300	782	1390	192	1730	724
Fencing	9330	2570	956	681	2570	1610	1160	905	1200	1200
Total £/ha	67600	22000	15800	10600	42300	19600	13000	5250	29500	18000

Table 4.11 **Weighted Mean Cost of Reclamation Schemes £/ha**

	Public Open Space <0.5 ha	1–2 ha	5–10 ha	>10 ha	Temporary	Agriculture	Woodland	Nature Conservation	Recreation	Mixed
Demolition	7600	3190	415	346	250	762	2180	76	2330	422
Disposal	3160	748	680	198	2570	435	104	57	981	739
Regrading	9768	1800	3980	4130	9840	3610	2740	1800	4570	4780
Drainage	8850	1050	671	945	2060	2040	1280	840	3721	2348
Topsoil	5920	2550	2080	44	2864	5856	0	26	6830	908
Cultivation	2570	825	471	1590	1090	1420	1190	502	1850	601
Seeding	1050	586	579	406	4310	604	254	68	1490	351
Planting	2310	2180	1990	758	4060	688	1390	192	1730	724
Fencing	5880	1440	641	681	1722	1260	870	905	936	1080
Total £/ha	47100	14400	11500	9100	28800	16700	10000	4050	24400	12000
Mean DOE Approved Costs for Clearance, Engineering, Landscaping, all sites.	52500	25400	11300	8250	21100	18400	12900	11400	25400	11900

Table 4.12 **Schemes restored with funds additional to DLG**

	No. of Sites with available information	% of Sites restored with funds additional to DLG: Local Authority	Other Source
POS <0.5 ha	8	25	13
POS 1–2 ha	11	45	18
POS 5–10 ha	7	29	29
POS >10 ha	5	40	20
POS Temporary	5	0	0
Agriculture	9	11	0
Woodland	7	29	0
Nature Conservation	3	66	0
Recreation	9	56	11
Mixed	20	55	20

4.6 Sources of Funding for Reclamation

For the majority of sites studied no significant funding additional to DLG was used in reclamation.

Table 4.13 shows the number of sites in each category where other funding was used as a percentage of the number of sites for which information was available.

Sources of additional funding other than local authorities' own budgets included the following:

Countryside Commission	(2 schemes)
National Coal Board	(2 schemes)
Water Authority	(1 scheme)
Sports Council	(1 scheme)
British Rail	(1 scheme)
Private landowner	(1 scheme)
Community Land Act funding	(1 scheme)
Housing Act funding	(1 scheme)
Income from sale of recovered land	(1 scheme)

The proportion of funding other than DLG ranged widely from very small percentages up to the entire cost where sale of recovered coal enabled the local authority to pay back the DLG.

PLATE 13 High quality, high cost urban reclamation with extensive use of trees, shrubs, furniture and hard surfaces at Croft Stairs, Newcastle.

PLATE 14 Naturalistic low-cost reclamation with extensive use of existing vegetation at Mill Bank, Kirklees.

PLATE 15 Innovative use of former gas holder tanks in formal public park in Hollicombe, Torbay.

PLATE 16 Naturalistic approach to creation of pond at Stourvale, Dudley.

4.7 Establishment Costs

The DLG scheme currently provides for costs of management of vegetation for up to five years from the completion of reclamation. Table 4.13 summarises those establishment costs approved as part of the DLG. Establishment costs were only claimed for 38% of the sites. Many local authorities commented that they were not aware that these initial maintenance costs were eligible for grant at the time the schemes were carried out. The proportion of more recent schemes where establishment costs were claimed would be higher. In some cases costs for the years immediately following restoration were included in landscaping contracts.

Information on the time period over which establishment costs were claimed was requested from local authorities and information was obtained for sixteen sites. The periods ranged from 1 to 5 years with a mean of 2.7 ± 1.7 years. Five of these sites were woodland and the mean period over which establishment costs were claimed for these was 3.8 ± 1.6 years. The average period for the remaining eleven sites was 2.2 ± 1.5 years.

The nature of the maintenance operations required and carried out during the establishment period is discussed in Section 5.0

Table 4.13 **Establishment Costs approved as part of DLG (£/ha)**

	No. of Sites	% of Sites	Mean	S.D.	Range
POS <0.5 ha	2	20	2180	802	1380 – 2980
POS 1–2 ha	4	36	1140	853	71 – 2280
POS 5–10 ha	5	71	406	201	113 – 629
POS >10 ha	1	20	49	–	–
POS Temporary	1	17	2780	–	–
Agriculture	2	18	128	15	112 – 143
Woodland	4	44	902	431	274 – 1470
Nature Conservation	3	75	412	336	124 – 884
Recreation	4	36	1500	752	927 – 2760
Mixed	12	50	931	476	87 – 1700

5. Management and Maintenance

This chapter describes the management and maintenance of the sites in the study. Management refers to the control and administration of the various afteruses, whilst maintenance describes the operations carried out.

The control and administration of sites is discussed in Section 5.1 and includes information obtained from local authorities on the organisation of management and maintenance, general strategies and administration costs. In the case of some afteruses, notably agriculture, part of the administration expenses incurred by local authorities were directed towards income generation. Income from sites may be used to offset some of the total management and maintenance costs. This aspect is discussed in Section 5.1.4.

Maintenance operations were assessed for the three main ground cover types present, namely agricultural grassland, amenity grassland and woodland. Other components such as water, scrub, hard surfaces and in one case arable crops were present on some sites, but it was not possible to consider the maintenance of these separately from the data available. Maintenance operations and costs for agricultural grassland, amenity grassland and woodland are described in Sections 5.2 to 5.4 and compared with standard costs and maintenance models compiled for these categories.

Limited information on both management and maintenance costs was obtained. A number of authorities did not have data available and others were unable to give a breakdown of costs on a site basis. The recorded variation in maintenance costs was expected as a wide range of factors were involved including site conditions; site location, size and access; labour organisation; machinery used etc. In practice costs were highly site specific. Nevertheless general trends in maintenance were evident from the data and these form the basis for the maintenance models.

Standard costs for typical maintenance operations carried out were derived from various sources including The Groundwork Trust (1986), Property Services Agency (1987), Nix (1986), The Scottish Agricultural Colleges (1986), Farm Contractor (1986) and local authorities involved in the study.

Maintenance models were compiled for each ground cover from an assessment of maintenance required and using standard costs. All costs were converted to 1986/87 prices as described in Section 2.5.

In order to assess the total maintenance cost for a particular afteruse, the proportions of different ground cover types present on the site were taken into account. The application of maintenance models to the sites and their limitations are discussed in Section 5.5.

5.1 Organisation and Administration

5.1.1 Responsibility for Management and Maintenance within Local Authorities

Information on the organisation of management and maintenance was obtained from seventeen local authorities. This varied considerably between county and district councils and also depended on the afteruse of the sites. As a general rule however the responsibility for management within county councils lay with a technical services department, whilst maintenance operations were carried out either by a direct labour organisation within a property services/ parks/leisure services department or by outside contract. Estates departments were also commonly involved, particularly where management required licence or tenancy agreements.

Responsibility for management within district councils was usually passed on to the parks/leisure services/ recreation departments who also carried out the work using direct labour. However in 30% of cases control was retained by the department responsible for reclamation and the parks department carried out maintenance operations on their behalf.

In addition to the use of direct labour and outside contractors for maintenance work, local authorities involved volunteers particularly on nature conservation and larger public open space sites.

5.1.2 General Strategies

Agricultural sites were usually retained and managed by local authorities. Agricultural land was sold by 14% of local authorities with experience of reclaiming land for agricultural use. In one case land had been leased for the purposes of reclamation and returned to the landowner on termination of the lease. Where land was retained by local authorities, most aimed to maximise income from agricultural land whilst retaining control via licences. In the longer term (usually after 5 years or more following completion of reclamation), county councils in particular aimed to establish tenancies. The purpose of this strategy was to ensure reclaimed land was sensitively managed, particularly in the early years after reclamation, by control of stocking rates and fertiliser inputs etc. Furthermore the council was in a better position to act if problems related to reclamation developed subsequently. However in a few cases there was a lack of attention to the maintenance requirement by the managing authority, and the licencing system does not enable the farmers maintaining the land to invest in long term improvements. Agricultural agreements are described further in Section 3.6.2.

Provision of public open space was seen as a district council function and sites restored to this afteruse by county councils were normally passed to the appropriate district council on completion. Exceptions to this were large areas reclaimed to "country park" style open space and linear sites such as old railway lines restored as footpaths or bridleways which crossed district council boundaries. In those cases control was normally retained by the county council.

Management strategies for amenity grassland sites including public open space and recreation were defined principally in terms of cutting regimes. A frequent cutting regime was adopted by all local authorities where sites were visually prominent in an urban setting or where it was required as a result of type or intensity of use. A less frequent regime was usually applied where the site was less prominent, was in a country location or had restricted use. One local authority was specifically changing to a regime with fewer cuts wherever possible to improve the nature conservation value of sites. In virtually all authorities the actual number of cuts was based on the organisation of maintenance schedules rather than the specific needs of a particular site. However in the case of larger public open space sites and country parks, strategies were more clearly set out in management plans. In contrast few formal recreation sites appeared to have well defined strategies.

The visual and amenity functions of woodland were considered to be the primary objective of virtually all schemes and management strategies were directed towards this. Only one local authority specifically included commercial production as a long term objective for some sites. The wildlife value of woodlands was recognised by all authorities as a further element and management to develop the wildlife potential was becoming increasingly important.

The general strategy for nature conservation sites was to involve local nature conservation trusts in the preparation of management plans and carrying out of maintenance tasks. One of the district councils had its own ranger service to carry out and supervise maintenance on nature conservation sites. However on one site no formal management structure was in existence.

5.1.3 Administration Costs

Limited information on administration costs was available for 33% of the sites. In most cases costs were given as very broad estimates only and varied widely between sites and local authorities. Some figures quoted were unrealistically low. Table 5.1 shows the mean totals and ranges for the various afteruses of sites. In relation to public open space, mean administration costs per hectare decreased considerably with increasing size of site from £2,023 on sites less than 0.5 ha to £87 on sites between 5–10 ha. Administration costs for other afteruses were more comparable and no significant trends may be detected when allowance is made for limitations of the data.

These costs may be compared with the average maintenance costs for the sites described in sections 5.2 to 5.4 below, and with published information. The expenses involved in owning and managing land apportioned to maintenance and repairs, statutory charges, insurance and management have been summarised for rural estates by Nix, Hill and Williams (1987). For county council owned estates, they reported that 55% of annual expenditure may be attributed to management costs, statutory charges and insurance and 45% to maintenance and repairs. Overall data from the sample sites appears to indicate similar proportions for the reclaimed derelict sites in the survey.

It should be noted that the administration costs in Table 5.1 include the expenses of preparing licence and tenancy agreements or letting for recreational use/other events. In these cases the costs are directed towards income generation and increased adminstration costs may be more than justified in terms of increased revenue.

5.1.4 Income

The potential for generating income applies to all afteruses to some degree, with the exception of the smaller public open space sites. However only in the case of agriculture was revenue separated out on a

Table 5.1 **Administration Costs**

Data for administration expenses including management salaries and expenses, professional fees, office expenses, insurances and statutory charges. Sites with available data. Note most of the figures quoted are very broad estimates only.

Afteruse Category	No. of Sites with Data	Total administration costs £ per ha	
		Mean	Range
POS <0.5 ha	3	2023	1963–2105
POS 1–2 ha	4	358	53–1150
POS 5–10 ha	3	87	57– 132
POS <10 ha		No data	
POS Temporary	2	139	37– 240
Agriculture		No data	
Woodland	5	176	8– 503
Nature Conservation	3	112	5– 320
Recreation	1	125	
Mixed	12	84	2– 427
All sites	33	315	2–2105

site basis for land let under tenancy or licence. Information was limited to 43% of let sites with an agricultural end use on part or all of the area. Income from agricultural grassland ranged from £30 per ha to £196 per ha, with a mean of £130. The figures include both licenced and tenanted land. For tenanted land, the average rent level for all crops, grass and rough grazing land in England is estimated in Nix (1986) as £102 per ha. This compares with typical rents of £85 per ha to £100 per ha on reclaimed land reported by one local authority. A higher mean income was found for sites in the study as most of these were let under licence. Income from licenses is normally higher than from tenancies because in the former, fertiliser etc. is supplied by the local authority.

No information was available on income from recreation sites even where the potential for charging for sports pitches existed. In most cases no income was derived from recreation sites nor had the possibility apparently been considered. However those sites with most potential for income invariably included those on which considerable additional investment had been made by the managing local authority. DLG was generally insufficient to enable the development of recreation sites without this additional input.

No income was recorded for public open space sites but priced publications, charges for special events and car parking noted for some large country parks may be used to offset high management costs. Charges for car parking were also made on one nature conservation site and the money collected by the resident warden.

Many woodland sites have the potential for income generation in the long term through sale of thinnings and timber. However no figures were available and the consideration of the income potential of woodlands is beyond the scope of this study.

5.2 Maintenance of Agricultural Grassland

Maintenance of agricultural grassland essentially involves the maintenance of the fertility of the sward and promotion of grass growth to achieve an economic return. This is achieved primarily through fertilisation of the sward, but other operations including weed control, rolling, chain harrowing and periodic reseeding are necessary to maintain vigour and prevent deterioration of restored land. In addition stock control is important on grazed swards.

The standard of maintenance applied will depend on the management arrangements, whether owner occupied, tenanted or licenced; the actual use of the grass sward, whether grazed, cut or both; and the production level.

5.2.1 Use of Agricultural Grassland

The areas of agricultural grassland ranged from less than 1 ha to 39 ha. 82% of the units were grazed or grazed and cut, with stock comprising primarily beef cattle and/or sheep. The remaining 12% were recorded as being cut for hay/silage only. There is no data as to whether this was due to a lack of water supply for stock; site location or farm organisation. Most of the agricultural units reclaimed did incorporate water supply for stock.

Reclaimed land was frequently located at some distance from the farmers' main buildings and often had a limited grazing season compared with the farmer's other undistributed land, as a result of poorer drainage and/or susceptiblity to drought. These factors tended to restrict use. Nevertheless the units commonly provided valuable accommodation land for livestock.

Horse grazing was recorded on three units, although this did not always have the full approval of the local authority. Horse grazing is not generally considered an appropriate use of reclaimed land because the uneven grazing habit of horses and damage from trampling lead to sward deterioration. Horses may also present a danger where there is public access to land. The use of an area for horse grazing may reflect the inhability of the local authority to rent out the land for a preferred agricultural use.

5.2.2 Operations Carried Out

Regular maintenance operations carried out were limited essentially to grassland fertilisation. On some units regular soil analyses were carried out to assess fertiliser requirements. Fertiliser was recorded as being applied annually to 46% of agricultural units in the study. The number of applications ranged from one in the majority of cases to three per annum on more intensively managed units. In addition many farmers spread farmyard manure or other organic material in large quantities where this was available. Such manuring was usually carried out on the farmer's own initiative and expense to improve soil fertility. Both licensee and tenant farmers applied organic manures in addition to the specified requirements of the local authority owners. In the case of licensees, this should not have occurred under the terms of the licence (section 3.6.2), but was of undoubted benefit to the land.

Further operations relating to soil and vegetation management were carried out on a very few units. These included subsoiling, rolling, reseeding, liming and weed control. Usually these operations were not annual but were carried out as and when required. Rolling, reseeding, liming and weed control were recorded more often during the establishment period than afterwards. Drainage was also installed on one site during the establishment period. This indicates a greater maintenance requirement on sites during establishment. Reseeding, for example, was recorded on 19% of sites during the establishment period. In most cases this was associated with failure of grass on part of the unit, although the reseeding of the entire area was carried out on one site. Similarly lime treatments were applied to areas where acid problems persisted after reclamation.

Other maintenance requirements on agricultural grassland include fence repair and checking and cleaning ditches, drains and water supply. Fence maintenance ranged from very minor repairs to gates to additional stockproof fencing (for example to enable sheep grazing) on the whole site. These operations were not annual, and costs were related more to the length of boundary, number of fields, etc. than to the area of the unit.

Harvesting of hay and silage and checking the welfare of grazing stock were largely left to the licensee or tenant, and little information was available for the sites in the study.

5.2.3 Cost of Maintenance

Table 5.2 shows the average costs of operations carried out on the units for which full data were available.

The figures quoted for fertiliser application are generally the combined cost of materials and spreading, as in many cases these costs were not separated. Contract tender sums tended to be a single figure for "supply and apply fertiliser". In a few cases the farmer spread fertiliser supplied by the local authority and figures relate to the cost of materials only. The cost of fertilising formed a high proportion of the total maintenance costs for agricultural grassland. Mean costs of fertilising during the establishment period were higher than afterwards, but the range in values was also large. The higher figures were generally associated with sites with two or three applications of fertiliser per annum, whilst the lowest figures correlated with sites where only one application of fertiliser was made per annum.

Data for the costs of other operations were more limited. The wide variation in these costs per hectare may be attributed to the degree of treatment and the proportion of the unit affected in each case.

Total annual maintenance costs for vegetation and soil were higher during the establishment period than afterwards, reflecting a greater maintenance requirement in the early years following reclamation.

Table 5.2 **Cost of Operations carried out: Agricultural Grassland**

Operation	Establishment			Annual		
	No. of Sites	Mean £/ha	Range £/ha	No. of Sites	Mean £/ha	Range £/ha
Drain	1	3534	–		No data	
Roll	1	13	–		No data	
Reseed	4	–	27–1368	1	118	–
Fertilise	10	112	52– 151	8	80	38–127
Lime	2	–	13– 68	1	27	–
Total vegetation & soil maintenance	7	141	76– 186	6	124	93–174

5.2.4 Standard Costs of Maintenance

Table 5.3 shows standard costs for operations commonly carried out on agricultural grassland. These standard costs have been used to compile annual maintenance costs for the model inputs described in Section 5.2.5.

5.2.5 Maintenance Models for Agricultural Grassland

The maintenance models for agricultural grassland are shown in Table 5.4, and include three input levels to take account of different uses and production levels. The components of the models are explained below and compared with actual maintenance operations and costs as described in Sections 5.2.2 and 5.2.3.

Fertiliser costs are based on three input levels; low, moderate and high. In practice fertiliser should be applied as necessary from soil analyses to maintain

Table 5.3 **Standard Costs of Maintenance Operations: Agricultural Grassland**

Operation	Standard Cost £/ha per operation
Subsoiling – shallow, flat lift or paraplow	32.00
– 0.45 m deep, 1.2 m centres	44.50
Ploughing – shallow 50 mm	23.25
– deep more than 230 mm	35.00
Rolling – flat	16.00
Chain harrowing	10.50
Fertilising inc. spreading and materials **per annum**	
– low input based on 75 kg N plus P&K	60.00
– moderate input based on 175 kg N plus P&K	116.00
– high input based on 275 Kg N plus P&K	197.00
Liming based on 5 t/ha including spreading	90.00
Weed control including spreading and materials	26.00
Reseeding including sward destruction by spraying; cultivations (ploughing, harrowing, rolling, seeding); seedbed fertiliser and spreading, seed cost	258.00
Harvesting hay – mowing	18.00
– turning x 4	56.00
– baling	39.60
– handling	17.40
Total:	131.00
Forage harvesting silage total	100.00
Fencing and Other Costs – nominal charge per annum	20.00

the fertility of the land and productivity of the sward. The low input system indicates that a minimum level of fertiliser is required to maintain any sward. The fertiliser would typically be supplied as a single application of compound including nitrogen, phosphate and potash (NPK) in the spring. The production level would be low intensity grazing or one hay crop with aftermath grazing. In the moderate input system, the fertiliser would be supplied in two applications, one in a compound fertiliser including NPK and one as straight N. Two cuts or a grazing/ cutting regime would be achievable. In the high input system, three applications of fertiliser would enable up to 3 cuts of silage per annum.

The majority of units with data correlated with the moderate input level during the establishment period. Mean fertiliser inputs after the establishment period were consistently lower. On several sites with annual data only, costs approximated to the low input level and all sites with full data sets showed the same trend towards lower annual inputs after establishment. The differences may be attributed to the need for higher inputs during the establishment period to build up soil fertility levels. It is also possible that some local authorities reduce inputs after the establishment period in order to ease the long term maintenance burden.

In addition to fertiliser, lime may be required to maintain an appropriate pH level as predicted from soil analyses. For the purposes of costing in the model, it is assumed that 5 t/ha ground limestone or equivalent is applied every 6 years.

Weed control costs are based on spraying once with a herbicide such as MCPA/MCPB/mecoprop and once with a dicamba mixture during a four year period.

The model incorporates a cost for flat rolling or chain harrowing, which are commonly carried out in the spring to invigorate the grass sward.

Table 5.4 **Agricultural Grassland Maintenance Models**

Annual Costs £ per ha	Low Input 75kg N/ha	Moderate Input 175kg N/ha	High Input 275kg N/ha
Fertilising	60	116	197
Rolling/chain harrowing	13	13	13
Spraying	13	13	13
Liming	15	15	15
Allowance for reseeding and subsoiling	26	39	61
Total vegetation & soil	127	196	299
Fencing & other costs, nominal charge	20	20	20
Total maintenance	147	216	319

Notes: 1. No harvesting costs included in the model.
2. Model costs intended to represent typical maintenance costs incurred by local authority letting agricultural grassland under licence.

Reseeding is recommended at intervals to maintain the quality of the sward for grassland production. The frequency of reseeding will depend on the production system and rate of deterioration of the sward. The models assume that reseeding will be required once every 10 years in the low input system but no additional soil treatments such as subsoiling would be carried out. In the high input system, allowance has been made for reseeding once every 5 years and for subsoiling to be carried out in appropriate circumstances. In the moderate input system, costs have been estimated to lie between the high and low input models.

With regarding to other maintenance costs, a nominal annual charge for maintenance of fences, checking and cleaning ditches, drains and water supply has been added.

Actual costs of weed control, liming, rolling and reseeding were recorded for very few units and no comparison could be made with the models. The lack of information is partly due to the fact that these operations were not carried out each year and local authorities were unable to apportion an annual cost. However many local authorities did not include these operations because they did not consider the necessity for soil improvement or reseeding. If the long term objective was to sell or establish a tenancy, then the local authority tended to carry out the minimum maintenance required. Responsibility for other operations would then pass to the tenant or owner occupier. Whilst this approach may cost less to the local authority, it may not be in the long term interest of maintaining agricultural production on reclaimed sites and could possibly lead to their deterioration.

Total maintenance costs for vegetation compared fairly closely with the low input model after the establishment period. Costs during establishment tended to be higher, mainly due to fertiliser (see above). Overall figures therefore suggest that local authorities tend to adopt a low input stategy, particularly after the establishment period. This is appropriate for some sites, for example in exposed locations where climatic factors are limiting and the surrounding agricultural land is of generally low productivity. However in many cases it is considered that local authority inputs should be more in line with the moderate input model to enable continuing beneficial agricultural use of sites reclaimed for this purpose.

No attempt has been made to include harvesting costs within the model although standard costs for harvesting operations have been given in Table 5.3. This is because the majority of units were grazed as well as cut and no cost information was available on either aspect of management. Harvesting costs and animal welfare in all cases were borne by the licensee or tenant.

Similarly no information was available on yields and value of the grassland to the farmer to enable comparison with actual and model inputs. However for all units except one, income from rents exceeded the maintenance costs for vegetation both during and after the establishment period. Rents were generally sufficient to cover both vegetation and fencing/other costs in most years. Income from rents was not normally enough to cover all management costs involved if administration expenses are taken into account.

5.3 Maintenance of Amenity Grassland

The length of grass for its designated use and visual appearance are the most important factors in the maintenance of amenity grassland for public open space. Regular cutting is the prime operation required but in addition, periodic fertilising and weed control may be necessary, especially on shorter grass, to maintain appearance and prevent deterioration of the sward. For recreation grounds additional maintenance requirements include surface aeration, light rolling, renovation and marking out.

All amenity grassland units were cut regularly but the number of cuts per annum varied between sites according to use. Three broad cutting regimes have been defined according to frequency of cut. These are shown in Table 5.5, together with the number of sites from each afteruse category cut under each regime.

Table 5.5 indicates that most of the small public open space sites, which were located in predominantly urban areas, were cut frequently but as the site areas increased (and location/access factors changed) the number of cuts per annum became more diverse. Overall a close cutting regime was adopted on 50% of public open space sites whilst paddock and long length were recorded on 29% and 21% of public open space sites respectively. Sites managed as paddock or long length tended to include larger areas of grassland.

As would be expected, all the recreation sites with grassland fell within the close mown category. The mean number of cuts per annum was greater than for public open space sites under the same regime, reflecting the more intense maintenance requirements of sports grounds.

Table 5.5 **Cutting Regimes: Amenity Grassland**

Number of sites is recorded in each category for the following cutting regimes:

'Close mown'	>8	cuts per annum
'Paddock'	3–8	cuts per annum
'Long'	1–2	cuts per annum

Afteruse	Close		Paddock		Long	
Category	No.	%	No.	%	No.	%
POS <0.5 ha	6	86	1	14	–	–
POS 1–2 ha	5	45	3	27	3	27
POS 5–10 ha	2	33	4	67	–	–
POS >10 ha	–	–	1	33	2	67
POS Temporary	3	50	–	–	3	50
POS Mixed Sites	8	53	5	33	2	13
Recreation Sites	9	100	–	–	–	–
Nat. Con. Sites	–	–	1	25	3	75

Mean Number of Cuts per annum from sites with data:

Close mown – POS Sites	14
Close mown – Recreation Sites	16
Paddock	5
Long	2

Differential mowing was carried out on nature conservation sites in order to maintain and encourage a wide variety of wildflower species. The long grass category here includes sites which were not mown, as a deliberate policy.

Information on the method of cutting was too variable to be represented, but machines used included the full range of cylinder and rotary pedestrian machines, strimmer, ride-on, 3 and 5 unit gang mower, and tractor-drawn flail and rotary mowers (Plates 17, 18). Disposal of cuttings was recorded on 3 sites as a once per annum operation after the last cut of the season. There was no recorded instance of using cuttings for hay.

PLATE 17 Tractor-mounted flail mower used in maintenance of grassland with low frequency of cutting.

PLATE 18 Gang mower in use on sports pitches.

After cutting, weed control, fertilising and reseeding were the most commonly recorded maintenance operations.

Weed control was recorded as being carried out on 27% of sites with public open space and over 55% of recreation sites. In general weed control was carried out on the same sites during the establishment period and annually. In the case of public open space it is unclear as to whether the data refers to general treatment of grassland or to selective weed control around amenity trees, paths and edges, etc. On sports pitches, herbicides were applied to the grassland areas to control broadleaved weeds as necessary.

Fertilising was carried out predominantly on recreation sites, with one or two applications per annum recorded both during the establishment period and afterwards. Fertiliser was also applied to some mixed end use sites and smaller public open space areas during the establishment period only.

Reseeding applied to 15% of sites with public open space during the establishment period, but few sites afterwards. Reseeding also occurred as an annual operation on recreation sites, usually where excessive wear required treatment rather than over the whole area. Cultivations recorded on some sites were invariably associated with the reseeding operation.

Other operations recorded for a number of sites mainly during the establishment period include subsoiling, drainage installation and liming. Fence repair, litter collection, amenity tree checks and regular safety and equipment checks were carried out at varying intervals on many of the sites. Marking was carried out on sports pitches as a regular operation where pitches were well used.

5.3.2 Cost of Maintenance

Table 5.6 shows the average costs of operations carried out on the units for which full data was available. Unit cutting costs varied considerably depending on a number of factors, including equipment used, size of area, shape of area, location of site and ground conditions (grass length, slopes, drainage, obstructions, etc.). Generally, however, small areas of amenity grassland were by far the most expensive to cut because of the need to use pedestrian machines or specialised mowing equipment. Where the equipment used had been specified, there was better agreement on unit cutting costs. For example, the cost of using a 5-unit gang mower ranged from £4 to £19 per hectare per cut, with a mean of £8.20. Flail mowing typically cost between £6 and £15 per hectare per cut, with a mean of £10.

Table 5.6 **Cost of Operations Carried Out: Amenity Grassland**

A. *POS by Afteruse Category*

Operation	POS <0.5 ha			POS 1–2 ha			POS 5–10 ha			POS >10 ha			POS Temporary			POS Mixed		
	No. of Sites	Mean	Range	No. of Sites	Mean	Range	No. of Sites	Mean	Range	No. of Sites	Mean	Range	No. of Sites	Mean	Range	No. of Sites	Mean	Range
Cutting	5	103	12– 150	7	37	9– 133	3	10	7– 15	No data			2	48	33– 63	7	27	6– 67
Disposal of Cuttings	–	–	–	–	–	–	1	8	–	No data			–	–	–	1	4	–
Weed Control	No data			3	42	31– 50	1	17	–	No data			No data			No data		
Other	3	198	158– 250	3	161	92– 217	No data			No data			No data			1	107	–
Total *per annum*	5	1502	320–2350	8	654	20–1692	4	65	47–100	No data			2	227	125–329	7	311	22–1068

B *POS by Cutting Regime and Location*

	All Close Mown			All Paddock			All Long			All Urban			All Fringe			All Rural		
Cutting	7	56	6– 150	7	14	6– 41	1	63	–	14	62	7– 150	9	20	6– 60	2	38	9– 67
Disposal of Cuttings	–	–	–	2	6	4– 8	No data			–	–	–	2	6	4– 8	No data		
Weed Control	2	48	46– 50	2	24	17– 31	No data			3	42	31– 50	1	17	–	No data		
Other	6	168	92– 250	1	175	–	No data			5	180	92– 250	1	107	–	1	175	–
Total *per annum*	17	804	55–2350	9	218	20–1460	1	125	–	14	841	55–2350	10	191	22–1068	3	693	20–1460

C. *Recreation Sites*

	Cost per ha per operation			Total Cost per ha per annum		
Cutting	7	23	9– 42	7	375	141– 781
Fertilising	3	165	114– 202	3	270	178– 404
Weed Control	–	–	–	4	25	16– 38
Reseeding	–	–	–	3	168	36– 330
Marking (pitch)	5	13	3– 40	5	166	40– 490
Aeration (pitch)	1	15	–	1	92	–

Note: Values derived from annual cost data only.

Costs from the establishment period where available were very similar to annual costs, except for reseeding, which was much higher during establishment.

All cost £ per ha.

For public open space, weed control costs in general did not separate grassland application from selective control around obstacles and along site margins. On some units, weed control costs were incorporated into 'other vegetation' maintenance costs. In Table 5.6 'other vegetation' maintenance costs include a variety of operations such as edging; maintenance of amenity trees; fertilisation, liming, and reseeding badly worn areas and use of growth retardant, which were carried out to varying degrees on a number of sites.

Unit cutting costs were recorded for 70% of the recreation sites in the study but the availability of data on the costs of other operations including fertilising, weed control, reseeding, marking pitches and surface aeration was more limited. The wide range in the cost of reseeding operations is due to variation in the proportion of pitches renovated.

5.3.3 Standard Costs of Maintenance

Table 5.7 shows standard costs for typical maintenance operations carried out on amenity grassland. These standard costs were used to compile annual maintenance costs for public open space and recreation models described respectively in Sections 5.3.4 and 5.3.5.

5.3.4 Maintenance Models for Public Open Space

Maintenance models for amenity grassland (public open space) are shown in Table 5.8. Six models have been prepared to cover the range of close mown, paddock and long cutting regimes and to take account of the area of units.

Maintenance regimes for public open space are highly site specific and will vary according to the aims and objectives for the site (Plates 19, 20). For example, enclosed urban sites may require intense maintenance in order to cope with high population pressures. Untidy areas and untreated margins may rapidly become a collecting ground for litter and encourage ill-use, leading to deterioration of the site. In other situations there may be opportunity to leave areas of longer or unmown grass which will encourage a more diverse range of species and habitats for wildlife.

Many amenity grassland sites include individual trees or groups of trees planted as standards and these will also require maintenance, in particular checking, protection, pruning, weed control and possibly mulching. Formal and informal sites may also require attention to paths, margins and bases of structures. On all sites allowance should be made for regular inspections (for safety purposes and illegal occupation as well as for site quality), litter removal and fence repairs (Plates 21, 22).

The item for miscellaneous vegetation costs in each model includes general and selective weed control; fertilising, disposal of cuttings where appropriate and amenity tree maintenance. Site inspections, litter removal and fence repairs are included on a site basis. Not all operations will be appropriate to every site. However it has been assumed in the models that the cost of one operation can be offset against another which is not required on a particular site.

In all cases the figures used are for annual operations after the establishment period, as there was little difference in both operations carried out and costs between the establishment and annual phases.

Table 5.7 **Standard Costs of Maintenance Operations: Amenity Grassland**

Operation		Standard Cost £/ha/operation
Cutting	– ped type/various for small sites	70
	– gang for larger sites	11
	– flail	15
	– gang + other for sports pitches	20
Sports Pitches:		
Fertilising	– total materials + spreading typ. per annum	160
Weed Control	– total herbicide + spraying for broadleaves in grassland mean per annum	25
Surface Aeration	– min. penetration 10mm; tractor	15
Rolling	– flat	11
Renovation	– reseed worn areas including raking, forking, seeding	35
Overmarking pitches		8
Other operations including litter removal, fence repair, regular inspections etc. Nominal annual charge for sites:		
POS < 2 ha		150
POS > 5 ha		80
Recreation sites		100

Annual cutting and total vegetation maintenance costs showed enormous variation between units due to factors discussed above. The use of six models for different cutting regimes and areas reduces this variation to some extent but cannot eliminate it and anomalies are bound to remain. For close mown units less than 0.5 ha in size, mean actual cutting costs were £922 per ha per annum and total vegetation management costs £1,010 per ha per annum. These figures compare favourably with the model costs of £840 and £1,015 respectively. Actual costs for the other categories were not as close to the model costs but there were only three or four units in each category with data for comparison. However for each category the general trend in maintenance costs was in accord with the model.

Table 5.8 **Amenity Grassland (POS) Maintenance Models**

Models based on annual costs after establishment period. Annual costs during establishment are similar, however an allowance may be added for fertilising once during establishment.

1. *Close Mown all units 0.5 ha or less*	£/ha/annum
Cutting 12× per annum small sites ped-type machine/various	840
Miscellaneous veg. costs incl. edges, amenity trees, weed control, fert. etc.	175
Total	1015
2. *Close Mown units 1–2 ha*	132
Cutting 12× per annum gang/tractor rotary	132
Miscellaneous veg. costs incl. edge cutting, amenity trees, weed control, etc.	220
Total:	352
3. *Close Mown units > 3 ha*	
Cutting 12× per annum gang	132
Miscellaneous veg, costs incl. selective weed control, fert., etc.	50
Total:	182
4. *Paddock Length units < 2 ha*	
Cutting 5× per annum flail	75
Miscellaneous veg. costs incl. weed control, disposal of cuttings, etc.	50
Total:	125
5. *Paddock Length units > 5 ha*	
Cutting 5× per annum flail	75
Miscellaneous veg. costs incl. weed control, disposal of cuttings, etc.	30
Total:	105
6. *Long Grass – all units*	
Cutting 2× per annum flail	30
Hay crop/disposal of cuttings	100
Miscellaneous veg. costs	30
Total:	160

Notes: For units with areas not falling into above categories, use mean of models e.g. Close Mown 0.5–1 ha – total £684/ha/pa.

For other operations including litter removal, fence repair, regular inspections etc. *add* £150/ha/annum for sites < 2 ha; £80/ha/annum for sites >5 ha.

5.3.5 Maintenance Model for Recreation Sites

The maintenance model for recreation sites is shown in Table 5.9. In practice the level of maintenance will vary considerably according to the standards of play required and the intensity of use. The model is suggested as the minimum necessary to achieve a reasonable quality pitch capable of sustaining weekly use. Pitches are assumed to be for football use. The more exacting requirements for some sports such as hockey have not been considered.

Table 5.9 **Recreation Sites Maintenance Model**

	Cost £ per ha per annum
Cutting 20× per annum	400
Fertilising – total materials and spreading per annum	160
General grassland weed control	25
Surface aeration 6× per annum	90
Rolling 2× per annum	22
Renovation worn areas 1× per annum	35
Overmarking pitches 26× per annum	208
Other operations inc. regular inspections, fence repairs, litter removal, selective weed control etc.	100
Total:	1040

Notes: 1. Similar maintenance requirements for establishment period and subsequent annual.
2. Drainage installation assumed at reclamation stage.
3. Costs do not include maintenance of structures and goal posts, changing facilities.

In addition to regular mowing, the model incorporates costs for fertilising, weed control, surface aeration, rolling, renovation, line marking and other operations.

Fertiliser costs are based on a combination of compound NPK applied in March to aid grass recovery and Nitrochalk in early August to give a boost before winter use (Plate 23). Additional fertiliser will be required on badly worn areas such as goal mouths during reseeding. Actual costs were higher than the model on those units where costs were recorded.

Herbicide application will be necessary to control broadleaved weeds and clover which have a low wear tolerance and consequently lead to a rapid deterioration of sward quality. Actual weed control costs were similar to the model but weed control was not carried out in all cases.

Regular aeration of grassed areas is required to penetrate and remove the surface mat and promote healthy growth and root development. Rolling would

PLATE 19 Close mown grassland in formal park at Hollicombe, Torbay.

PLATE 20 Varied mowing regimes of grassland in large public open space at Parson's Meadow, Wigan.

PLATE 21 Litter collection is important in maintaining the appearance and safety of sites.

PLATE 22 Lack of attention to edges. Maintenance of these areas is particularly important but on many sites this incurs high costs because of the need to use hand-held machines for difficult areas along walls and fences. Individual standard trees also require separate treatment.

normally be carried once during the summer and once before the main winter season begins. The limited information on these operations was in accord with the model on those units where recorded.

Renovation will be required each year on areas of high wear such as goal mouths and involves raking, forking, fertilising and seeding a limited proportion of the pitch. Reseeding was recorded for 50% of the units and mean costs were higher than the model. However it is not clear whether the high reseeding costs recur at this level annually or apply only to the year for which data was obtained.

Overmarking of pitches for play will depend on the intensity of use. Overmarking was recorded on 50% of units and in most cases mean annual costs tended to be lower than the model. This was largely attributable to lower actual cost per operation than given in the standard costs.

With regard to other operations, the model includes a nominal annual charge for regular pitch inspections, litter removal, fence repairs etc. Costs do not include maintenance of structures such as goal posts, changing rooms, pavilions etc. which may form a high proportion of total maintenance costs but are site specific. It has been assumed that drainage is carried out as a capital cost at the reclamation stage, although drainage to the standard required is not normally eligible for DLG (Plate 24).

Overall the model appears to give a realistic representation of maintenance operations and costs on a typical winter grass sports pitch. The lower total actual costs compared with the model reflects the omission of some required operations in the maintenance regime.

5.4 Maintenance of Woodland

5.4.1 Operations Carried Out

Woodland planting had been carried out on 70% of the total sites in the study and ranged from small or dispersed groups of trees less than one hectare in size to blocks of trees between 1 and 10 hectares. The majority of woodland was planted for amenity purposes, either visual only or with public access, and the nature conservation element was also considered on many sites. No sites were recorded as being purely commercial forestry, although four units were classified as 'productive woodland'.

The maintenance operations carried out largely reflect this amenity use of woodland and the young age of the trees in the survey. In addition trees spaced at 1½ to 2m will require maintenance in order to encourage successful establishment and healthy growth. Regular maintenance operations during the establishment period included replanting and weed control and to a lesser extent, fertilising and pruning. These operations were also recorded on some units under annual maintenance. Mulching, liming and thinning were carried out on a very few units only, whilst other operations included staking, tying, erosion control, mowing of fire breaks and hedge trimming.

Replanting was recorded as being carried out on 48% of the woodland units and was commonly noted as an annual operation throughout the establishment period. Although the proportion replanted was not recorded in many cases, a comparison of replanting costs with the cost of the initial planting for 6 of the woodland end use sites in the survey suggested that, on average, over one-third of the initial planting required replacement during the establishment period. This indicates a high proportion of tree failures on reclaimed derelict sites. After the establishment period, replanting continued to be recorded on some units. It is not clear whether this was continued beating up due to tree failures or additional planting for amenity purposes. On a few sites the local authority had increased the area of woodland when additional funds had become available for tree planting.

Chemical weed control was recorded for 52% of the woodland units (Plates 25, 26). This operation was usually carried out annually during the establishment period and occasionally more than once per annum. Chemical weed control continued as an annual cost on 20% of the units after establishment. Hand weeding was recorded on fewer sites and sometimes occurred in addition to chemical weed control. The number of occasions hand weeding was carried out ranged from once during establishment to twice per annum. Fertiliser applications varied similarly between units.

Other maintenance requirements on woodland areas include fence repairs, checking and cleaning ditches and drains, and road maintenance (Plate 28). Fence repairs in particular were recorded as being required on some 22% of the woodland units. The cost of maintaining fences on small woodlands can be very high in proportion to their area.

5.4.2 Cost of Maintenance

The average costs of tree maintenance operations carried out are shown in Table 5.10. For all operations the figures show a wide variation in average cost per hectare between units. Reasons for these variations include the size and age of the planting, proportion of the area treated, type of material and method or equipment used. Replanting costs for example will depend on the number of

PLATE 23 Sports pitches require intensive maintenance in order to sustain regular use. On this site fertiliser was being spread by hand.

PLATE 24 Good drainage is essential for winter pitches. Here sand slits are being installed in football pitches.

failures, type of trees used in beating up, and method of planting. With regard to weed control, it was noted from site visits that spot treatments carried out did not always apply to all trees. Also on many sites, costs were combined into a single figure for chemical and hand weeding.

Total annual costs of vegetation and soil management were slightly higher during the establishment period but not significantly so. It would be expected that the differential would be much larger, as expensive operations such as replanting and weeding should be confined largely to the establishment period and few woodland stands had reached the stage where pruning and thinning costs formed a significant proportion of annual costs after the establishment period. This suggests that woodland is generally slow to establish on reclaimed derelict land and requires more attention after the establishment period than conventional woodland planted on undisturbed sites.

Table 5.10 **Cost of Operations carried out: Woodland**

Operation	Establishment			Annual		
	No. of Sites	Mean £/ha	Range £/ha	No. of Sites	Mean £/ha	Range £/ha
Replant	20	157	8–417	2	48	17– 78
Chemical weed	20	99	7–248	7	80	15–167
Hand weed	4	58	42– 75	2	106	44–167
Fertilise	4	19	4– 44	3	28	15– 43
Lime	1	37	–	No data		
Prune	No data			4	51	11– 83
Other	3	–	1– 29	2	–	28–255
Total vegetation & soil maintenance	22	260	45–715	14	184	21–526

5.4.3 Standard Costs of Maintenance

Table 5.11 shows the standard costs of maintenance operations on woodlands. These have been used to compile annual maintenance costs for the model inputs described in Section 5.4.4.

Table 5.11 **Standard Management Costs: Woodland**

Operation	Standard Cost £ per ha per operation
Replanting – 10% of initial	139
Weed Control – spot weed @ 6p/transplant	150
Fertilising – total materials & spreading	184
Pruning – 1000 trees per ha	288
Thinning – 1500 trees per ha	275
Fencing and Other Costs – nominal charge p.a.	
a. small/dispersed blocks <1 ha	100
b. blocks 1 – 10 ha	50

5.4.4 Maintenance Models for Woodland

Woodland maintenance models for both the establishment period (years 2–5 after planting) and for years 5–20 are shown in Table 5.12.

The allowance for replanting in the model is indicated as 10% of the initial planting cost. Trees which die in the first year should be covered by the planting contract, and in general the reclamation contract should incorporate an allowance for ensuring a minimum survival rate at the end of the establishment period. In practice this does not appear to cover the high failure rates reported for the reclaimed sites.

Mean actual replanting costs during establishment were much higher (4.5 times higher) than the model and formed approximately 60% of total annual maintenance during the establishment period. High replanting costs were especially associated with smaller blocks of woodland and sites in urban locations. This is not unexpected as edge effects are greater in small blocks and damage from vandalism is usually more common in urban situations. Nevertheless it is considered that actual replanting costs were excessive in many cases and the continued beating up of tree failures over several years is not a cost effective approach.

Table 5.12 **Woodland Maintenance Model**

Establishment Period	Cost £ per ha
(Years 2 – 5 after planting)	
Replanting once 10% initial	139
Weed Control/Fertiliser for 3 years (either regular weed control on fertile sites or combination of fertiliser/less intensive weed control on less fertile sites)	951
Total for 4 years:	1090
Mean annual during Years 2 – 5:	273
Maintenance Years 5 – 20	
Pruning/Brashing/Thinning	563
Total for 15 years:	563
Mean annual during Years 5 – 20:	38
For fencing and other costs *add* £100/ha/annum for small/dispersal blocks <1 ha; £50/ha/annum for blocks 1 – 10 ha.	

Weed control and fertiliser are typically required to varying degrees during the establishment period, depending on competition from grass and broadleaved weeds and the nutrient status of the substrate.

In contrast with replanting, combined actual costs of chemical weed control, hand weeding and fertiliser were less than half (46%) of the model cost for these operations. However overall costs of vegetation management (excluding fencing) during the establishment period were similar to the model.

Overall the figures for the establishment period suggest that local authorities were carrying out woodland maintenance but were directing funds more

PLATE 25 Tree establishment and growth will be enhanced by good maintenance. Control of weed growth in particular is important on fertile sites.

PLATE 26 It is essential that those involved in maintenance are properly trained and equipped. Here careless use of herbicide has severely damaged this young tree.

PLATE 27 Standard trees are expensive to buy, plant, protect and maintain. Maintenance is often neglected and trees may suffer serious damage such as illustrated here.

PLATE 28 The block plantings of whips on this site are well protected and maintained and have established and grown well.

towards replacement of failures than encouraging establishment and growth of the initial planting. In some cases adverse site conditions and vandalism were responsible for the high proportion of failures but good reclamation practice and subsequent maintenance should alleviate much of the need for substantial replanting. Establishment and growth were observed to be variable on many sites and there is a case for reconsidering management strategies in these situations.

After the establishment period, pruning of some or all of the trees in the woodland planting may be necessary to produce the desired shape of tree and improve visual appearance. Pruning will also enhance timber values where productive woodland is an objective. Similarly thinning operations should be carried out as necessary. For productive woodland, Helliwell (1984) cites as common practice reducing trees planted at 2m × 2m spacing to about 1000 per hectare before the branches of adjacent trees have become interlocked. The model incorporates a nominal annual charge for pruning/brashing and thinning operations between years 5 and 20. It was not possible to compare this with actual costs as no figures for the same period were available. On some sites no maintenance had been carried out since the end of the establishment period.

Various other maintenance costs are involved in woodland management including fence repairs, checking firmness of plants, and condition of tree guards, fire precautions, access roads etc. Fence repairs in particular can form a high proportion of total annual costs, particularly on small or dispersed areas of woodland planting. When applying the woodland model to sites, two levels for these other costs were used depending on whether the woodland area covered less than 1 ha or was in blocks between 1–10 ha in size.

5.5 Application of Maintenance Models to Sites

The sites commonly combine more than one ground cover type, particularly in the case of mixed end use sites. The model cost of maintenance for a particular afteruse has been calculated by summing the model costs of maintaining the ground cover types present in proportion to their occurrence, and averaging the total over the whole site to give a mean cost per hectare.

In the case of nature conservation sites, models for amenity grassland and woodland have been applied where appropriate. In practice these require modification, for example fertiliser inputs are inappropriate on sites where floristic diversity is important and similarly weed control is likely to be restricted to selective treatments in certain circumstances. Woodland management inputs may be considerably reduced if areas of tree failure are left to develop naturally as open areas rather than replanted and if the rate of woodland establishment is unimportant. The latter strategy may also be appropriate for some woodland end use sites.

Nature conservation sites typically embrace a wide range of habitats. The few sites in the survey incorporated natural colonisation of three different substrates by ground flora, scrub and woodland each with their own maintenance requirement. Water areas were also involved. Consequently maintenance costs can vary enormously. The widespread use of voluntary labour for maintenance tasks is a further complicating factor and applies to all sites, with the probable exception of agriculture.

The site models are restricted to maintenance and repairs and do not take into account administration costs (Section 5.1.3) or income (Section 5.1.4). No attempt has been made to include administration costs because of wide variations in the data and the lack of accurate estimates from local authorities or in published information. Information on income was similarly limited and could not be incorporated practically into the models. Costs for wardening and interpretative facilities are also absent. In practice these may form a high proportion of total management costs particularly on larger public open space and nature conservation sites. For example the cost of wardening and administration on one site was estimated by the local authority at approximately £320/ha/annum.

All these factors should be borne in mind when considering the overall cost effectiveness of management as discussed in Chapter 7.

6. Present Use and Performance of Sites

The present use and performance of sites was assessed largely on the basis of observations made on site visits together with information provided by local authority officers. Use and performance were assessed under five main criteria.

1. Safety
2. Land use compatability
3. Visual benefit
4. Amenity use
5. Nature conservation value

For each site a score out of 20 was calculated for each criteria. These scores were then combined to give an overall site score out of 20. The methods of evaluation for each criteria are outlined in 6.1.

There are disadvantages of such a scoring system. These include the following:

- Several of the criteria are interdependent.
- The scoring procedure is to an extent arbitrary and subjective.
- Some of the criteria and values are very difficult to score.

In addition the system only take account of the direct benefits of the sites themselves. Indirect benefits such as stimulation of economic development were beyond the scope of this study. The system takes no account of the limited options which may be available for some sites, particularly small areas of urban dereliction, or the maximum potential score achievable in any particular location.

However, the system provides a systematic and standard procedure for ranking sites in terms of use and performance. This approach produces a more consistent evaluation, repeatable by different assessors to give similar results, than would be achieved by a purely subjective assessment.

6.1 Evaluation of Main Criteria

6.1.1 Safety

Local authorities, and indeed all landowners, have obligations under the Occupiers Liability Acts 1957 and 1984 to persons visiting land in their ownership. The 1957 Act defines the common duty of care towards visitors as 'a duty to take such care as in all the circumstances of the case is reasonable, to see that the visitor will be reasonably safe in using the premises for the purpose for which he is invited or permitted by the occupier to be there' (Occupiers Liability Act 1957). The 1984 Act extends this duty of care to all those not covered by the 1957 Act.

In scoring sites for safety we considered that a major hazard existed if visitors were exposed to risk of injury through normal use of a site. If a hazard existed but exposure would not arise through normal use of the site this was regarded as minor.

6.1.2 Land Use Compatibility

This criteria was assessed in terms of the appropriateness of the use of the site in relation to other land uses in the vicinity.

6.1.3 Landscape Value

The value of a site in its landscape was assessed in terms of its visibility, the viewing population (the number of persons who would be expected to see the site on a daily basis), and the visual quality of the site.

6.1.4 Amenity Value

This was an evaluation of the use of the site based on an assessment of the user groups benefitting from the site, the numbers using the site on a daily basis, the suitability of the site for a range of activities, adverse effects of use and the quality of management of the site with regard to users.

6.1.5 Nature Conservation Value

This was assessed on the basis of the value of the site as a 'green link', the presence of native trees and shrubs, the diversity of trees and shrubs, the use of existing vegetation in the reclamation scheme, the presence of native herbaceous species, the contribution of unplanned native species, and the presence of water.

6.2 Evaluation of Other Factors

In addition to the main criteria described in 6.1 other factors were also assessed during site visits. These were:

— Site maintenance
— Public pressure
— Physical and chemical factors
— Vegetation quality

These factors did not contribute to the overall scores for sites.

6.2.1 Site Maintenance and Public Pressure

Evaluation of site maintenance consisted of assessment of the quality and level of maintenance.

Public pressure was assessed in terms of the type and density of housing nearest to the site, the accessibility of the site from housing, the presence and accessibility of site to schools and use of the site as a through route.

6.2.2 Physical and Chemical Factors and Vegetation Quality

These parameters were assessed on the basis of the management units described in Section 2.4.2.2. Physical and chemical factors comprised drainage, landform limitations, soil type and depth, and evidence of chemical toxicity or nutrient deficiency.

For assessment of vegetation quality, the vegetation on the sites was classified into the following categories:

Agricultural Grassland
Amenity Grassland: Close mown public open space
Close mown sports use
Paddock length/long grass
Trees/Shrubs

The assessment criteria varied for each depending on the characteristics of the vegetation and the requirements of use. In general the vegetation was scored for appearance, density of cover, and problems of weeds. In the case of sports pitches, resistance to wear and playing quality was also assessed. Wildlife value was assessed for paddock length/long grass and trees and shrubs. Visual impact was also assessed for trees and shrubs.

6.3 Results – Site Assessments

The assessments of the use and performance of sites by afteruse are shown in Table 6.1. Each of the criteria assessed are discussed in turn.

6.3.1 Safety

The majority of sites did not present any hazards to users and where these did exist they were generally minor. There was little difference between afteruse categories in terms of safety scores with the exception of recreation sites which scored rather low. Problems observed included a missing barrier on a footbridge crossing a stream with vertical sides and concrete bed, unrestricted access to a railway line, dangerously high walls and damaged fencing around a children's play area. In most cases the hazards had been recognised at the time of reclamation and fencing installed or other measures taken to protect users (Plate 29). However, due to vandalism or lack of maintenance the protection had been rendered ineffective.

6.3.2 Land Use Compatibility

The uses of all sites examined were considered to be appropriate to their locations (Plate 30) with the exception of two sites restored to temporary open space pending further development. One of these was an area restored to woodland with a long term aim of industrial development. The site was surrounded on three sides by housing but no provision for access or use by the community was made. The site was surrounded by a 2 m high chain link and barbed wire fence which had been damaged to gain access.

Table 6.1 **Assessment of Use and Performance of Sites – Mean Scores for Afteruses**

	Public Open Space (POS)					Agric.	Con.	Nat. Wood.	Rec.	Mixed
	<0.5 ha	1–2 ha	5–10 ha	>10 ha	Temp.					
SAFETY	19.5	19.5	17.9	20.0	20.0	18.6	18.8	18.9	16.5	18.1
LAND USE COMPATIBILITY	20.0	20.0	20.0	20.0	15.0	20.0	20.0	20.0	20.0	20.0
VISUAL BENEFIT	13.7	12.0	15.2	14.7	13.0	13.9	13.2	14.4	13.3	15.9
AMENITY USE	13.0	13.6	15.0	15.5	10.2	8.8	13.9	9.4	14.1	13.2
NATURE CONSERVATION	2.9	10.6	14.1	13.2	4.7	4.7	14.3	11.6	3.1	10.3
TOTAL	13.8	15.1	16.4	16.7	12.6	13.2	16.1	15.0	13.4	15.5

PLATE 29 Some sites included dangerous features. In most cases the hazards were recognised and precautions taken.

PLATE 30 The land use of most reclaimed sites was compatible with their surroundings. In this example the reclaimed agricultural grassland in the foreground was readily incorporated into the farming regime on adjoining fields.

The other site was also temporary open space pending industrial development. The site was poorly finished at the time of reclamation with remnants of old fences left on site. The site could not be distinguished from derelict land in the vicinity.

Both sites had the appearance of total neglect and reversion towards dereliction.

6.3.3 Visual Benefit

There was little distinction between the afteruse categories with regard to the overall visual benefit provided by reclaimed sites. Within each category there were considerable differences between sites. Sites providing high visual benefit were typically prominent city or town centre sites or sites adjacent to main roads and railways visible to high numbers of people (Plate 31).

Those sites providing little visual benefit were typically raised former lagoons or reservoirs with the majority of the site not visible from the surroundings, areas in flat landscapes surrounded by trees or hedgerows, or remote sites. In two cases the sites were poorly managed and unattractive (Plate 32).

6.3.4 Amenity Use

The amenity use of sites varied considerably between afteruses. The larger public open space sites provided the highest values while agricultural, woodland and temporary public open space sites were of low value.

Agricultural sites were typically relatively remote and access was normally restricted to the farming owner, tenant or licensee (Plate 34). In the case of woodland sites these were also typically not close to high densities of population. However in some cases when plantings have matured, are less susceptible to damage and more suitable for amenity use, it is possible that use may be encouraged and they may be of more benefit in this respect.

The public open space sites with low scores for amenity use were typically open grassed areas, little used other than for exercising dogs. No provisions were made for other uses.

The site achieving the highest score in the smallest size category of public open space was a city centre site finished to a high quality with mass planting of shrubs with seating and open grassy areas encouraging a high level of use. In this case 60% of the costs of the scheme were funded by DLG. The remainder was provided by the local authority. In the next size category the site achieving the highest score was an urban park constructed on the site of a town gas works, again finished to a high quality encouraging intensive use. Of the larger public open space sites those achieving the highest scores were those providing for a wide range of activities and typically included informal kickaround areas, open grassy areas and planting with footpaths. Some included specific facilities such as children's play equipment, trim tracks, cycleways and separate bridleways (Plate 33).

The nature conservation site achieving the highest score was Hazelslade Local Nature Reserve in Cannock Chase District where the nature conservation and educational use was well integrated with fishing, and informal play and picnic areas. This was made possible by the presence of a warden at the site (see 7.1).

Of the recreation sites, that with the lowest score was an area adjacent to a school playing field intended as an extension to the field but which could not be used as a result of a dangerous retaining wall. The site with the highest score was a playing field linked to other existing facilities on the edge of an urban area heavily used for informal recreation.

The poorest mixed sites with regard to amenity use were those in agriculture and woodland as would be expected from the performance of sites with these as single end uses. The most valuable mixed use sites for amenity use were a nature park comprising well integrated nature reserve and public open space areas and a mixed agricultural, public open space and woodland site forming part of a larger country park on the edge of an urban area.

6.3.5 Nature Conservation Value

Nature conservation values varied widely between the various categories of afteruse. As would be expected sites with a nature conservation end use had the highest average score. The average scores for public open space sites were lowest for small sites increasing to higher scores for the sites above 5 ha. Agricultural and recreation sites had low average scores. Woodland and mixed use sites were intermediate.

The public open space sites less than 0.5 ha in size were largely urban comprising mown grass with a few standard trees with little of conservation value (Plate 36). Those sites with most conservation value in this size category were those with significant areas of tree and shrub planting. Of the larger public open space sites those with lowest scores were largely close mown grass with standard trees. The proportion of this type of site decreased with increasing size of site. Sites with most conservation value were those where

PLATE 31 High scores for visual quality were given to prominent sites which formed attractive features in the landscape.

PLATE 32 Site with low visual quality.

PLATE 33 Sites which attained high scores for amenity use included those offering a range of facilities. Provision of a children's play area has enhanced the use of this site.

PLATE 34 In some cases sites had little amenity use and provided only visual amenity. Most agricultural sites fell within this category.

a high proportion of existing vegetation had been retained as part of the reclamation scheme. Such sites usually had a wide range of habitat types including short and long grass, scrub and woodland and water features such as ponds or streams (Plate 35).

Agricultural sites were typically uniform grassland grazed by stock or cut for silage with little conservation interest. Some sites were of slightly higher value, normally as a result of tree and hedge plantings as part of the reclamation scheme.

Recreation sites typically comprised sports pitches of close mown grass of very low conservation value. Some sites were of increased value where significant tree and shrub planting had been carried out or where some areas of longer grass were present in areas not used for sports.

Woodland sites were generally considered to be of relatively high conservation value but habitat diversity was usually low.

The nature conservation values of the mixed use sites followed the pattern of the respective single use sites. Sites with low scores included public open space of close mown grass, agricultural grassland and allotments. Sites with high scores were those including specific nature conservation end uses combined with public open space.

6.3.6 Overall Scores of Use and Performance

The afteruse categories with the highest average overall scores for use and performance were public open space sites about 5 ha in size. These sites tended to be of high visual benefit and scored highly for amenity use and nature conservation value. The lowest average overall score was that for temporary public open space where scores for land use compatibility, amenity use and nature conservation in particular were low. Agricultural sites also had a low overall average score as a result of low amenity use and nature conservation scores. Both recreation sites and public open space sites of less than 0.5 ha also had low overall average scores with particularly low scores for nature conservation value.

6.4 Results – Management Unit Assessment

As described in Section 6.2.2 assessment of physical and chemical factors, and vegetation quality was carried out on the basis of management units based on ground cover types.

6.4.1 Physical and Chemical Factors

The factors assessed were as follows:

Drainage	: Surface waterlogging Wet depressions Impermeable soils
Landform	: Steep slopes Complex slopes Settlement hollows
Soil	: Top soil texture Top soil depth Sub soil texture Total soil depth Compaction Stoniness
	Chemical toxicity
	Nutrient deficiency

Table 6.2 summarises the extent to which physical or chemical factors were resulting in problems of management.

Assessments were made in the context of the actual use of the land and the potential achievable as a DLG reclamation scheme. For example, in the case of agricultural land the potential normally achievable following reclamation was permanent grassland. Assessment of the effects of physical and chemical factors on management was on the basis of this potential. For public open space the land was usually required to support amenity grass and tree plantings and assessments were made on that basis.

In assessing the severity of problems, the extent to which normal management operations would be affected was taken into account. In agricultural grassland, a problem was considered to be major if mechanised operations were severely restricted over the whole area and/or grazing opportunities were limited (Plate 37). Shallow soils or moderately steep slopes did not generally present a significant problem for the management of permanent grassland although some limitations of below average yields or restricted access may remain. Such sites were assessed as having no problems and could be successfully maintained to a high standard (Plate 39).

On amenity grassland the assessment depended on the use of the site, as to a certain extent management practices may be adapted to site conditions without detriment to use. For example, a confined badly drained area within large open space which could be readily avoided by cutting machinery, and which would have negligible effects on public access and use was not considered to be a problem. In contrast a similar area of poor drainage within a picnic area or playing field was assessed as a localised major problem. Problems were scored as major where physical or chemical limitations occurred extensively across the unit, preventing management operations and adversely affecting use.

For tree and shrub sites, problems were considered major if a large proportion (approximately 30% or more) of the total planting was adversely affected and

PLATE 35 Diversity of habitat and retention of existing vegetation resulted in high scores for nature conservation value.

PLATE 36 Site with low nature conservation value. Such sites were common in urban areas.

Table 6.2 **Physical and Chemical Limitations for Management**

Limitation		Extent of Problem	% of Units Affected: Agric. Grassland	Non-Agric Grassland	Trees/Shrubs
DRAINAGE	Surface Waterlogging	Major	14.3	10.8	4.7
		Local major	7.1	3.1	3.1
		Minor	35.7	18.5	17.2
		None	42.9	67.6	75
	Wet Depressions	Major	0	1.5	1.6
		Local Major	3.6	0	1.6
		Minor	14.3	20	7.8
		None	82.1	78.5	89
	Impermeable Soils	Major	3.6	7	0
		Local major	3.6	0	0
		Minor	25	10.8	18.8
		None	67.8	82.2	81.2
LANDFORM	Steep Slopes	Major	3.6	0	3.1
		Local Major	0	5	0
		Minor	28.6	16.9	15.6
		None	67.8	78.1	81.3
	Complex Slopes	Major	0	0	0
		Local major	0	0	0
		Minor	7.1	4.6	0
		None	92.9	95.4	100
	Hollows	Major	0	0	0
		Local Major	3.6	0	0
		Minor	3.6	12.3	4.7
		None	92.8	87.7	95.3
SOIL	Topsoil Texture	Major	0	15	4.7
		Local major	0	0	0
		Minor	21.4	15.4	17.2
		None	78.6	83.1	78.1
	Topsoil Depth	Major	0	0	3.1
		Local major	0	0	0
		Minor	46.4	12.3	10.9
		None	53.6	87.7	86
	Subsoil Texture	Major	0	0	1.6
		Local major	0	0	0
		Minor	46.4	13.8	20.3
		None	53.6	86.2	78.1
	Total Depth	Major	0	0	3.1
		Local major	0	0	0
		Minor	50	10.8	9.4
		None	50	89.2	87.5
	Compaction	Major	0	4.6	0
		Local major	0	0	0
		Minor	39.3	20	7.8
		None	60.7	75.4	92.2
	Stoniness	Major	3.6	0	0
		Local major	0	0	0
		Minor	14.3	6.2	7.8
		None	82.1	93.8	92.2
TOXICITY		Major	0	0	3.1
		Local major	0	0	0
		Minor	7.1	7.7	14.1
		None	92.9	92.3	82.8
NUTRIENT DEFICIENCY		Major	0	0	0
		Local Major	0	0	0
		Minor	25	7.7	4.7
		None	75	92.3	95.3

trees were not likely to survive (Plate 9). Limitations were assessed as localised major when smaller areas were damaged, although growth over a larger area may be affected. Minor limitations were those which were unlikely to affect the long term survival of plantings (Plate 38).

Since these assessments were made on the basis of subjective observations on one site visit it is probable that limitations were to some extent underestimated. This is reflected in the assessments of vegetation quality.

6.4.1.1 Drainage

Surface waterlogging was a common problem in agricultural grassland units. 57% of units were affected, 14% of units to a major extent. 32% were

PLATE 37 Major problem of poor drainage on agricultural land. Extensive surface waterlogging severely restricts both agricultural operations and grazing, leading to colonisation by rushes and rank grasses and deterioration of the land.

PLATE 38 Minor problem of chemical toxicity on woodland unit. Acid leaching out of the underlying colliery spoil has caused localised death of vegetation.

affected by impermeable soils but problems were generally minor.

Surface waterlogging was also the most common drainage problem in non-agricultural grassland with 32% of units affected. In 11% of these the problems were major.

Tree and shrub units did not suffer from drainage problems to any significant extent.

Table 6.3 **Management of Units**

Limitation		Agric. Grassland	% of Units Non-Agric Grassland	Trees/ Shrubs
Management	Very Poor	3.6	1.6	3.1
	Poor	14.3	6.3	15.6
	Adequate	25	39.1	41
	Good	39.3	45.3	41
	Excellent	14.3	7.8	0

These drainage problems usually resulted from a combination of adverse landform, and soil characteristics which were not individually of major significance.

6.4.1.2 Landform The restored landforms caused few problems of significance. There were some problems resulting from steep slopes and hollows.

6.4.1.3 Soil Some problems of topsoil and subsoil texture and depth were recorded but these were generally of minor significance in relation to the use of the land. The same was true of compaction and stoniness problems. Agricultural grassland units were affected to a greater extent than non-agricultural grassland and tree and shrub plantings. However the flexibility of management of agricultural land was often limited by soil depth.

6.4.1.4 Toxicity Problems of chemical toxicity were rarely observed and were considered to be a major problem in only one unit of tree/shrub planting.

6.4.1.5 Nutrient Deficiency: Nutrient deficiency was common in agricultural grassland but only to a minor extent (see also Section 6.4.3.1). Problems were rare in non-agricultural grass and tree/shrub plantings.

6.4.2 Management Factors

Information regarding the quality of management is summarised in Table 6.3. An adequate level of management was considered to be the minimum level of attention necessary to maintain use of the site without a decline in its condition. Good scores and

Table 6.4 **Vegetation Quality in Management Units**

Agricultural Grassland		% of units	Non-Agricultural Grassland: Close Mown		% of units	Non-Agricultural Grassland: Paddock/Long		% of units	Trees/Shrubs		% of units
Crop Pattern	Uniform	59	**Sward Pattern**	Uniform	71.7	**Sward**	Excellent	11	**Establishment**	Uniform	42
	Patchy	41		variable	28.3	**Suitability**	Satisfactory	87		Patchy	58
							Not satisfactory	2			
Crop Colour	Good	67	**Sward Colour**	Good	82.6				**Growth**	Uniform	42
	Variable	29.6		Variable	17.4					Patchy	58
	Poor	3.7									
Sward Density	Dense	63	**Sward Density**	Dense	73.9						
	Variable	11		Variable	4.4						
	Open	26		Open	21.7						
Weed Problem	None	11	**Weed Problem**	None	26.1	**Noxious Weed**	One sp.	16.7	**Noxious Weed**	One sp.	19
	Minor	74		Minor	63	**Problem**	Two sp.	19	**Problem**	Two sp.	9.4
	Major	15		Major	10.9		Three sp.	31		Three sp.	21.9
							Four sp.	19		Four sp.	19
							Five sp.	2.3		Five sp.	9.4
Weed Dist.	Uniform	7.4	**Weed Dist.**	Uniform	58.7	**Weed Dist.**	Uniform	7.1	**Weed Dist.**	Uniform	28
	Patchy	22		Patchy	21.7		Patchy	23.8		Patchy	25
	Local	59		Local	10.9		Local	59.6		Local	17.2
	None	11.6		None	8.7		None	9.5		None	29.8
Legume Cover	<10%	48	**Legume Cover**	<10%	58.7	**Legume Cover**	<10%	52.4			
	>10%	52		>10%	41.3		>10%	47.6			
Legume Dist.	Uniform	15	**Legume Dist.**	Uniform	43.5	**Legume Dist.**	Uniform	16.7			
	Patchy	59		Patchy	47.8		Patchy	61.9			
	Local	19		Local	4.4		Local	4.8			
	None	7		None	4.4		None	16.6			
						Wildlife	Minor	7.1	**Wildlife**	Minor	14.1
						Value	Intermediate	69	**Value**	Intermediate	53.1
							High	28.6		High	31.3
									Visual Impact	Low	3.1
										Intermediate	21.9
										High	75

PLATE 39 Well restored agricultural land with stock proof fencing and water supply maintained to a high standard by the local authority. Such sites are readily licenced for grazing at competitive rents.

PLATE 40 Where sites are unmanaged they may degrade to a state of secondary dereliction.

above indicated that management provided the potential for improved performance since initial reclamation. In contrast management was assessed as poor or very poor where lack of attention to maintenance was likely to lead, or had led, to deterioration of the reclaimed land (Plate 40). The quality of management of most units was considered to be adequate or good (64% of agricultural grassland, 84% of non-agricultural grassland and 82% of tree/shrub units). 18% and 19% respectively of agricultural grassland and tree and shrub units were considered to be poorly or very poorly managed. 8% of non-agricultural grassland units were in these categories. Management of some agricultural and non-agricultural grassland units was considered to be excellent (Plate 39).

6.4.3 *Vegetation Quality*

Information on vegetation quality is summarised in Table 6.4. Since the basis of assessment for the ground cover types was different, each is discussed in turn.

6.4.3.1 Agricultural Grassland Most of the agricultural grassland units were characterised by uniform, dense crops of good colour. However a significant number of units had patchy crops (41%), of variable or poor colour (33%) and variable or open swards (37%). Weed problems were common and were major at 15% of sites. In most cases these weeds were localised in distribution. Legume cover was greater than 10% on approximately half the sites but the distribution was typically patchy.

6.4.3.2 Non-Agricultural Grassland The quality of close mown grassland units was generally high and problems of sward appearance and weeds were less common than in agricultural grassland. Legume cover was greater than 10% on 59% of the units and they were generally well distributed through the swards.

Management units comprising paddock length and long grass were generally of a quality suitable for their end use, usually of informal recreation. Noxious weeds were present in a high proportion of the units but were usually confined to localised areas. 29% of the swards were considered to be of high nature conservation value.

6.4.3.3 Tree/Shrub Plantings Establishment and growth in tree and shrub plantings were frequently patchy and weed problems were common. The majority of plantings were considered to be of significant wildlife value, 31% of units to a major extent. The majority of units were of high visual significance.

6.4.4 *Management Units – Scored Assessments*

The scored assessments for management units are summarised in Table 6.5. The maximum score for each parameter is 20. Assessment of the physical and chemical status of the management units of the various ground cover types gave similar results, as did the overall management of the units. With regard to overall quality of vegetation, scores for close mown amenity grass and tree and shrub plantings were generally higher than those for agricultural grassland, sports turf and paddock/long grass.

Table 6.5 **Assessment of Management Units**

Parameter			Non-Agric Grassland			
		Agric. Grassland	Close Mown POS	Sports Turf	Paddock/ Long	Trees/ Shrubs
PHYSICAL & CHEMICAL FACTORS	Mean	17.2	18.3	17.3	18.2	18.1
	SD	1.8	1.6	1.9	1.3	2
	Range	13.5 – 20.0	13.0 – 20.0	13.5 – 20.0	13.5 – 20.0	10.0 – 20.0
MANAGEMENT	Mean	15.7	15.5	15.7	14.9	14.4
	SD	2.9	2.1	1.9	2.3	2.5
	Range	8.6 – 20.0	11.4 – 20.0	12.9 – 20.0	8.6 – 20.0	8.6 – 17.1
VEGETATION	Mean	11.7	15	11.4	11.7	14.1
	SD	4.4	2.8	4.1	3.1	3.4
	Range	5.0 – 20.0	10.0 – 20.0	5.6 – 17.5	1.7 – 18.4	4.3 – 20.0

7. Cost Effectiveness

Cost effectiveness may be defined as the achievement of strategic objectives within a generally acceptable level of expenditure. In assessing cost effectiveness we have taken into account the costs of carrying out reclamation and of maintaining sites and the benefits arising from the restored land. Figures can be derived for the costs of reclamation and maintenance of derelict sites as described in Sections 4.0 and 5.0 of this report. The value of completed sites is less easy to define. Where a financial return is gained from the land, as for example agricultural sites, this could be included in the assessment of performance. However, since agricultural sites were not directly maintained by local authorities, information on yields was not available. Some information on income from rents etc. was obtained. For most end uses such as public open space, nature conservation and amenity woodland there is usually no direct financial benefit. This is recognised under the DLG scheme where land retained by local authorities for amenity or public open space use is regarded as having a nil aftervalue. The assessment of benefits in these cases may be based on a subjective assessment of visual attributes, use and site quality. For the purposes of this study the assessment method described in Section 6.0 was devised.

This section discusses the relationships between the capital costs, maintenance costs and performance of the afteruses and gives examples of sites which illustrate some of the principles.

7.1 Capital Costs and Performance

Section 4.0 details the capital costs of schemes in the various afteruse categories. In comparing capital costs with performance the most appropriate costs are the weighted mean costs of reclamation per hectare given in Table 4.11, since these take account of the frequency with which the various components of reclamation costs are incurred. Figure 7.1 compares these costs with the total performance scores described in Section 6 and summarised in Table 6.1. It can be seen that there is wide variation between the cost effectiveness of the various categories of scheme measured in these terms. The most cost effective sites were those restored to nature conservation where the low capital costs connected with this type of scheme were associated with high overall benefits. These were not limited to nature conservation but covered a range of amenity uses. A good example is the Hazelslade Local Nature Reserve restored by Cannock Chase District Council (Plate 41). This 12.6 ha site was the site of a former colliery and was affected by mining subsidence. A reclamation scheme based on a consultant's report which made full use of the existing vegetation and conservation value of the site was implemented. The overall cost of the scheme was £8,500 per ha which included acquisition costs of £4,400. The site contains a wide diversity of habitats including open water, marsh and swamps, woodland, meadow and pasture and is of high nature conservation interest. It is also an important and well used amenity providing for a range of activities including picnicking, walking, fishing and wildlife observation and it is a valuable educational resource used by local schools. Part of the site also provides low intensity grazing land for a local farmer.

Large public open space sites were also cost effective as a result of the economies of scale associated with reclaiming large areas and the high visual and amenity benefits associated with these sites. The Stourvale scheme carried out by Dudley Metropolitan Borough Council is a good example of an economical scheme providing considerable benefits to the neighbouring population (Plate 42). This reclamation scheme involved 6.8 ha of land adjacent to the River Stour. The site has a history of coal working. Reclamation included treatment of mine shafts and adits, some regrading, seeding and planting in selected areas and construction of footpaths, kickabout and children's play areas. Retention of existing vegetation was an important feature of the scheme. The overall cost was £4,700 per ha. The site is surrounded by housing and is a valuable amenity area. The footpaths are well used as is the children's play area. This site also provides wildlife habitat including river banks, a pond with well developed marginal vegetation, riverside meadow and other grassland, scrub and developing woodland.

Woodland sites were also relatively cost effective due to the low capital costs of reclamation, in particular the use of *in situ* rather than imported soils.

The least cost effective afteruse category in terms of the relationship between capital costs and

Figure 7.1 **Capital Costs of Restoration and Performance of Sites**

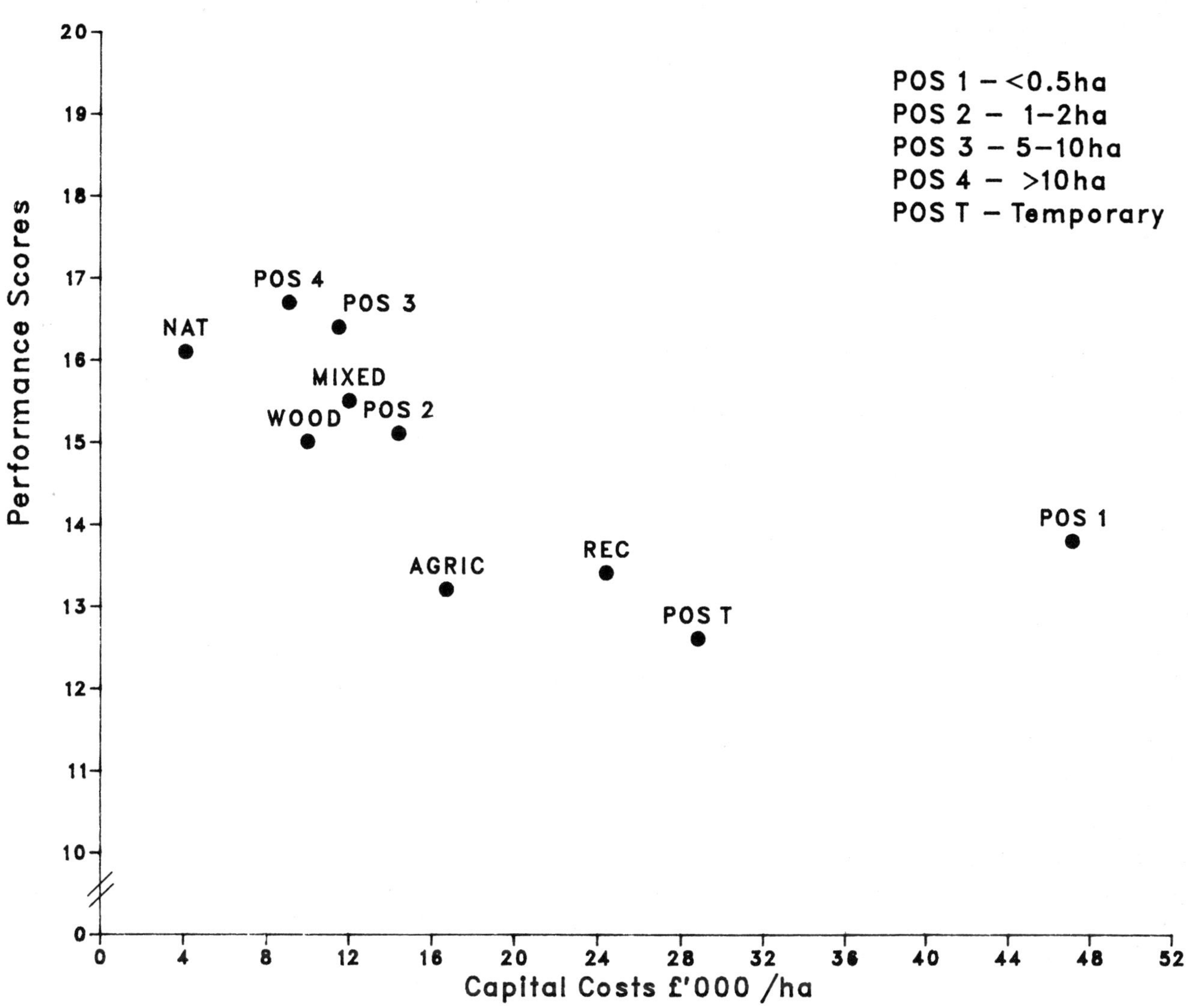

PLATE 41 Hazelslade Local Nature Reserve in Cannock Chase Distrct. A successful reclamation where nature conservation has been integrated well with amenity, educational, recreational and agricultural uses.

PLATE 42 Stourvale, Dudley. Extensive use of naturally regenerated grassland and scrub combined with selective regrading and planting has produced an attractive site of high amentiy value.

Table 7.1 **Establishment Costs**

Afteruse	1 Mean Model Costs/ha All Sites	2 Mean Model Costs/ha Sites with Data	3 Std. Costs of actual maintenance per ha	4 Std. Costs of maint. as % of model costs	5 Score	6 Effectiveness
POS <0.5 ha	743	829	967	117	13.8	2.6
POS 1–2 ha	414	411	438	107	15.0	2.1
POS 5–10 ha	272	272	302	114	13.9	2.6
POS >10 ha	240	ND	ND	ND		
POS Temp.	553	553	401	73	12.6	1.8
Agriculture	229	264	231	88	13.4	2.5
Nature Conservation	207	204	143	70	16.7	2.0
Woodland	320	324	328	101	15.2	2.5
Recreation	952	938	607	65	13.3	1.9
Mixed	265	267	203	76	15.5	2.4

Table 7.2 **Annual Costs**

Afteruse	1 Mean Model Costs/ha All Sites	2 Mean Model Costs/ha Sites with Data	3 Std. Costs of actual maintenance per ha	4 Std. Costs of maint. as % of model costs	5 Score	6 Effectiveness
POS <0.5 ha	679	809	1094	135	13.1	2.6
POS 1–2 ha	340	326	363	111	15.0	2.1
POS 5–10 ha	177	197	298	151	13.1	2.5
POS >10 ha	179	ND	ND	ND		
POS Temp.	514	514	426	83	12.6	1.8
Agriculture	207	250	142	57	12.75	2.25
Nature Conservation	170	ND	ND	ND		
Woodland	112	ND	ND	ND		
Recreation	949	953	661	69	13.6	1.9
Mixed	177	186	211	113	15.5	2.4

performance were public open space sites of less than 0.5 ha as a result of the very high capital costs per hectare associated with these small urban sites. Temporary public open space sites are recreation sites also showed low cost effectiveness as a result of the high costs and relatively low performance of these sites.

7.2 Maintenance Costs and Performance

The costs of maintaining reclaimed derelict sites are discussed at length in Section 5.0 of this report. Standard costs for maintenance operations and their derivation are also described in that section.

Tables 7.1 and 7.2 show the costs of maintenance of the sample sites. Table 7.1 shows the costs during the establishment phase and Table 7.2 the continuing costs after the establishment phase. Column 1 of each table shows the mean maintenance costs for all sites derived using the standard costs and maintenance models described in Section 5.0. Column 2 shows those mean model maintenance costs for those sites where information on maintenance was available.

In column 3 of the tables the mean costs of maintaining the sample sites where management information was available are shown calculated by applying standard costs to the maintenance operations actually carried out. These costs are expressed as a percentage of the model costs for the same sites in column 4 of each table. This provides a measure of the extent to which the maintenance requirements of sites as described in the models of Section 5 were carried out.

Column 5 of each table shows the mean performance scores for the sites in each afteruse category as described in Section 6. Column 6 is a measure of the extent to which the upkeep of the sites was considered to be effective in ensuring that the performance of the sites was maintained. This was assessed at site visits and measured on a scale of 0–3.

It can be seen that in general the maintenance input for public open space sites tended to be equivalent to or greater than that described by the models. In the case of agricultural sites the maintenance inputs decreased from 88% during the establishment phase to 57% subsequently. This may not necessarily be entirely a result of a reduction in maintenance effort but may reflect increasing hidden inputs by occupiers. The maintenance input for recreation sites was low during both the establishment phase and subsequently.

In Figure 7.2 these percentage values are plotted against the measure of the extent to which the management of the sites within each afteruse category was effective. It can be seen that there is a general relationship between the effectiveness of management and the extent to which maintenance requirements of sites were carried out.

Where maintenance costs per annum are 100% or more of the model requirements for a particular afteruse, it would be expected that mean effectiveness scores would approach the maximum value 3.0. In practice the mean effectiveness score achieved is actually less than the potential maximum since it is unlikely that maintenance of all sites in a particular afteruse category will be fully effective. Since there is no finite upper limit on maintenance costs the mean input as a % of model costs can increase to above 100%. It can be seen that the maximum mean scores achieved are in the region of 2.4 – 2.6 corresponding to maintenance inputs of approximately 100–150% of model requirements.

It should be emphasized that these maintenance costs are gross costs. In the case of agricultural land income from rents and licence agreements must be set against these costs. As discussed in Section 5.0 this income was generally sufficient to cover the maintenance costs of sites but not the full cost of managing the land when administration and other costs were included. Some other afteruses produced income. For example at Hazelslade Nature Reserve described in 7.1, income was obtained from fishing permits and grazing rent.

Although this relationship between maintenance effort and effectiveness is evident at the level of the afteruse categories, if compared with performance scores then it is not possible to demonstrate such general relationships. Site specific factors other than maintenance inputs influence the performance scores of sites. These include visibility, level and range of use by the public and nature conservation value. Thus no direct relationship between the level of maintenance and the performance of the sites was observed.

However, particular examples of sites where economical maintenance was combined with high performance may be mentioned. A good example of cost effective management of public open space is Normanby Brickworks, a site reclaimed and maintained by Cleveland County Council (Plate 43). This 7.4 ha site forms part of a larger area of public open space on the edge of the built up area of Teesside. It is linked to another restored brickworks (Ormesby) by a footpath along a disused railway line. The site includes open grassed areas, scrub, woodland picnic areas, a trimtrack and car park. The grassland maintenance within the site is varied with close mowing restricted to picnic areas and path edges. The remainder of the grass is maintained as paddock with two cuts per year with a tractor mounted flail. Some areas are left uncut to encourage scrub growth. New planting included a high proportion of fast growing species such as Alder, Willows and Poplars resulting in rapid establishment and reducing the need for weed control. A Manpower Services Commission team and local schoolchildren are involved in maintenance of the site. The site provides a popular, heavily used amenity area in the Cleveland urban fringe.

The importance of careful design and implementation in reducing maintenance costs while providing high levels of benefit should be emphasized. Good examples were Knights Pool in Macclesfield where a 1.3 ha site including 1.0 ha of water in a former mill reservoir, was treated for safety reasons (Plate 45). Where possible the pre-existing naturally colonised trees and shrubs were retained and require little maintenance. A small area of close mown grass is maintained at the part closest to surrounding housing where a footpath enters the site. This path provides a through route for pedestrians and is well constructed and surfaced requiring little maintenance. The pool is used by fishermen. The retention of existing vegetation, particularly trees and shrubs, provides a most effective way of keeping maintenance costs low since it is in the early stages of their establishment that the highest costs are incurred. The costs of maintaining established trees and shrubs are low.

Several other sites where relatively low maintenance requirements were coupled with a high degree of benefit may be cited. These included Springfield Lane, Sandwell; Stourvale and Buckpool Wedge, Dudley; and Anglezarke and Leicester Mills Quarries, Lancashire (Plates 47 and 48).

7.3 Capital and Maintenance Costs

The capital costs of reclamation schemes were discussed in Section 4 of this report and maintenance costs in Section 5. In comparing these capital costs with maintenance costs the model maintenance costs are of most relevance since these represent the standardised costs of site maintenance eliminating variation between local authorities.

Fig. 7.3 shows the relationship between the weighted mean capital costs compared with the annual model maintenance costs for each category of afteruse. It can be seen that in the case of public open space there is a direct relationship between these two costs. It is likely that some of the factors affecting the cost of reclamation, i.e. size of site and ease of access, also affect the cost of maintenance. It is important to note that these maintenance costs are gross costs and do not take into account any income which may be derived from sites. This applies particularly to sites in agricultural use.

The costs for most other categories of site are closely grouped with some exceptions. Recreation sites were expensive to manage in relation to their capital costs.

Figure 7.2 **Maintenance Input and Effectiveness**

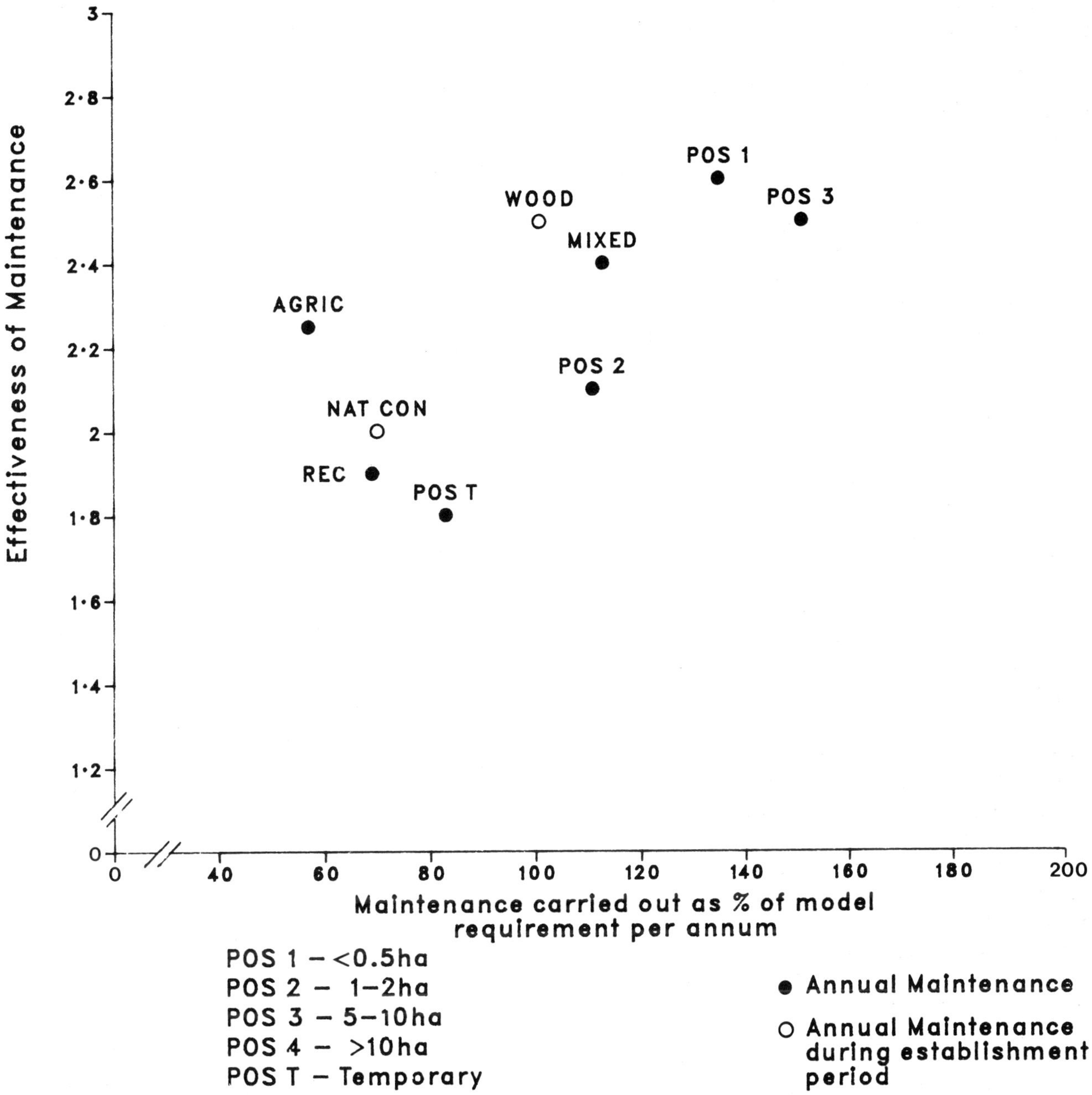

The model used assumed that these sites were maintained to a level which would provide for a reasonable standard of weekly use. In practice the actual level of maintenance of the sites in the survey was lower than this and close to the general relationship shown by the other categories of site. In the case of agricultural sites the maintenance costs were relatively low in comparison to capital costs. The cost effectiveness of agricultural sites in this respect is due to the more extensive nature of agricultural operations compared to maintenance of the other types of site. In practice net maintenance costs for agricultural sites in so far as the local authority owners are concerned are reduced below this level since income from licensees does, to a considerable extent, cover the cost of maintenance (see Section 5). Where appropriate the income from agricultural land included within a reclamation scheme may be sufficient to provide revenue to offset the costs of maintenance of other landscape components such as public open space, and woodland (Plate 46).

For example, a former colliery site restored to agriculture by a county council included 18.3 ha of agricultural grassland with small areas occupied by woodland and an access track. The site was let on an annual licence. In 1987 14.4 ha of this site was grazed by sheep and 3.9 ha cut for silage. The local authority applied fertilizer to the site three times per year and also incurred other costs including maintenance of water supply, fencing and soil sampling and analysis. The total annual maintenance cost for the grassland area was £2,255. The licence income to the local authority was £3,396. The annual cost of maintaining the woodland during the establishment period was £327. No woodland maintenance had been carried out after the establishment period. It must be remembered that these costs do not include administration.

Another former colliery site, again restored by a county council, comprised 26 ha of agricultural grassland, 14 ha of amenity grassland and 29 ha of woodland. The agricultural land was again let on an annual licence. The local authority annual maintenance costs of £2,680 included fertilizing, liming, and fence repairs. The licence income to the local authority was £3,465. No details of amenity grassland and woodland maintenance costs were available for this site.

Within site categories no relationship between capital and maintenance costs was detected. This resulted from the general lack of detailed costs of maintenance operations on a site specific basis. Reliance on standard costings makes any analysis of the data less sensitive at the individual site level.

Figure 7.3 **Capital Costs of Restoration and Maintenance Costs**

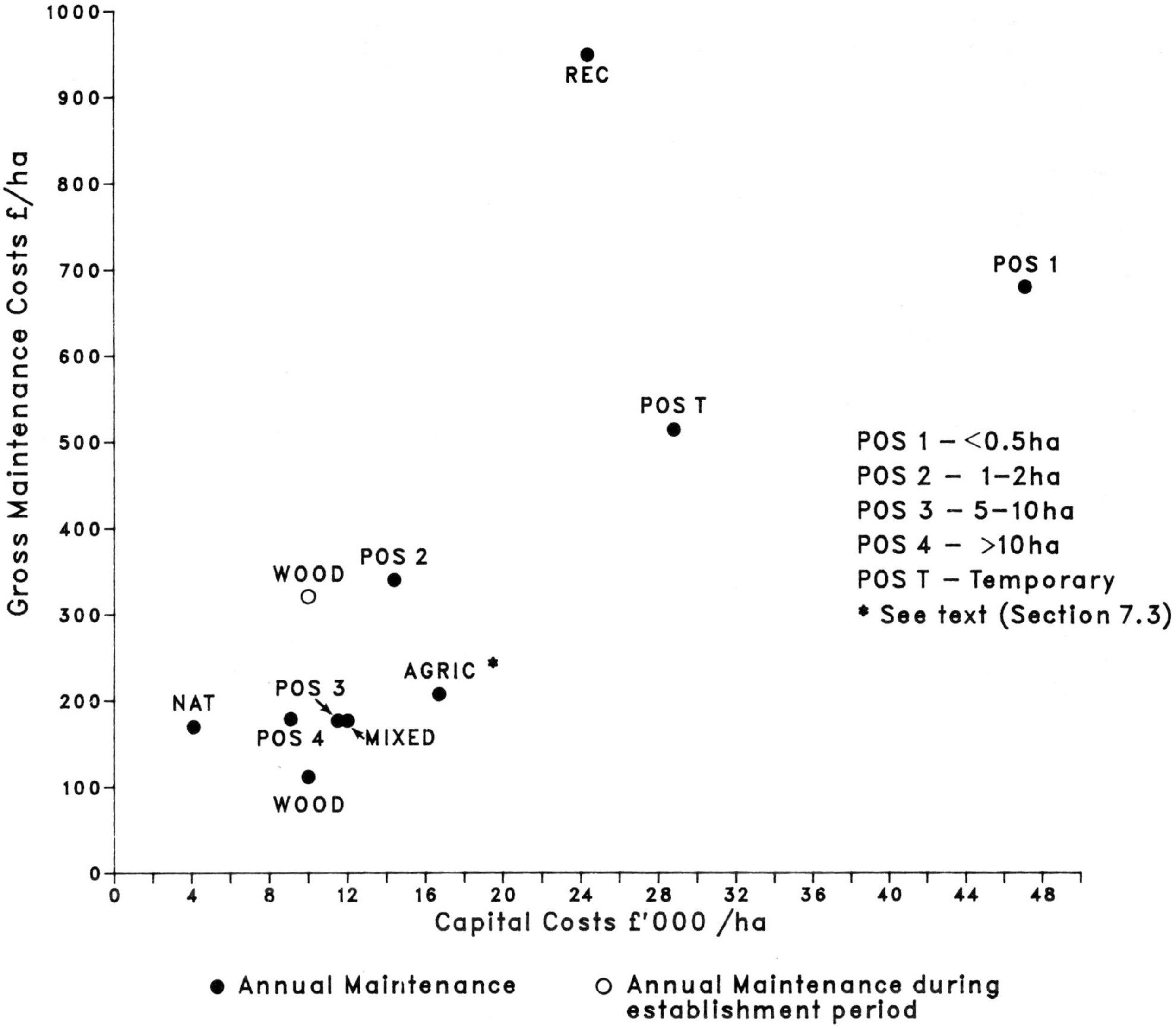

PLATE 43 Normanby Brickworks, Cleveland. Economical maintenance combined with high amenity use make this a very effective reclamation.

PLATE 44 Campsall Clay Pits, Doncaster. Provision of fishing facilities enables use of lakes by local angling club, which both increases site benefits and generates income.

PLATE 45 Knights Pool, Macclesfield. A well designed scheme where high levels of maintenance are restricted to areas of intensive use.

PLATE 46 Agricultural land as a component of mixed end use sites can produce income to offset the costs of maintaining other land. The reclaimed areas of Bestwood Country Park, Nottinghamshire includes agricultural grassland, public open space and woodland.

PLATE 47 Derelict land which has been colonised naturally by vegetation can often be reclaimed to a beneficial afteruse at low cost by improving access, providing footpaths and carrying out selective treatment. Site at Buckpool, Dudley.

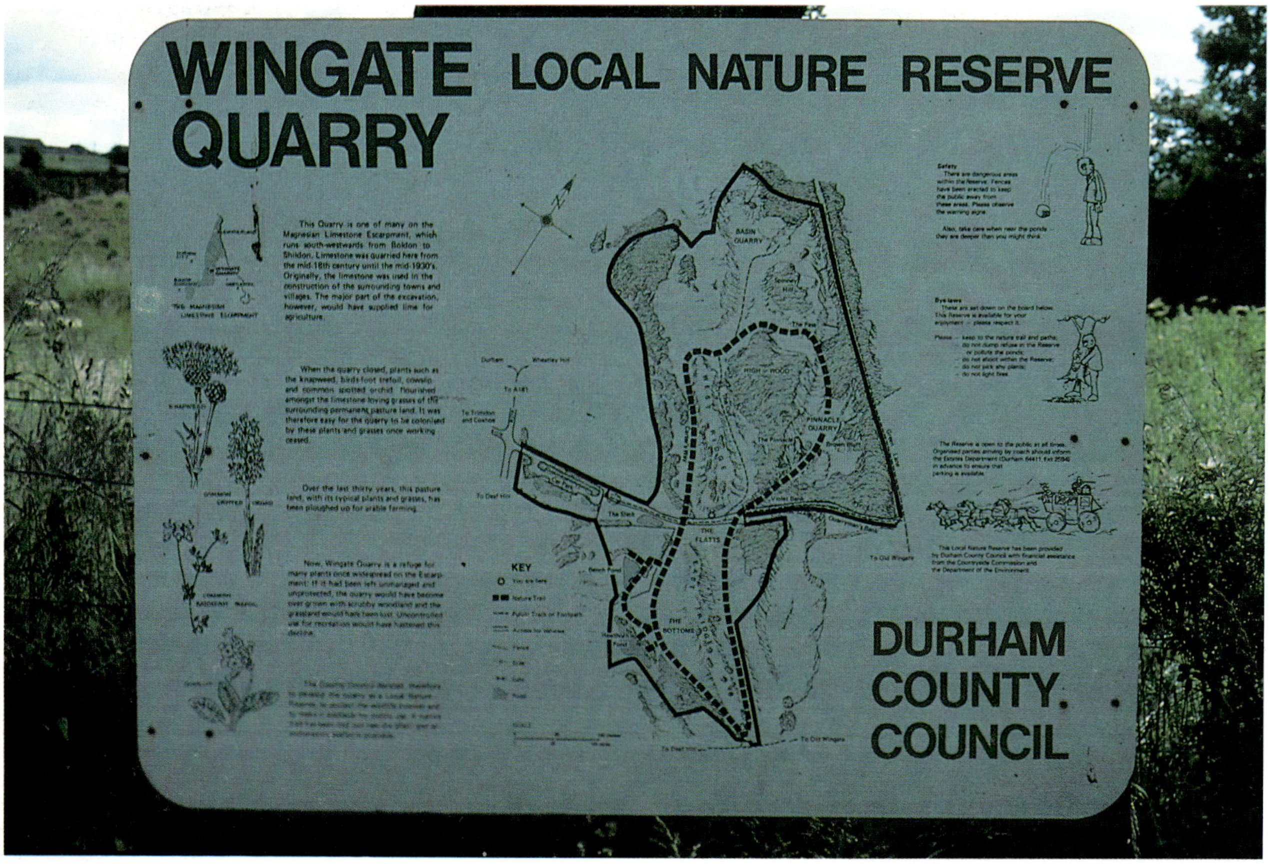

PLATE 48 Provision of descriptive and interpretative material increases public interest in and awareness of sites.

8. Conclusions

The preceding sections of this report have described the research carried out during this project and detailed its findings. This section sets out the conclusions drawn under the three main headings of:

— Annual maintenance costs and operations.

— Cost effective land management strategies.

— Capital and maintenance costs and performance of sites.

8.1 Annual Maintenance Costs and Operations

If restored sites are to continue to perform effectively in the long term and not degrade to a state of secondary dereliction then they must be managed. Section 5.0 of this report discussed in detail the maintenance operations typically carried out by local authorities on the various categories of sites examined, and described standard models for maintenance. These operations and models were costed. Comparison of the models with actual maintenance of particular ground cover types on an overall site basis indicated that, in general, local authority management was at a level appropriate to the current use of the sites. However there were certain notable exceptions where maintenance levels were not appropriate.

Maintenance of agricultural land tended to be at a low level particularly after the intitial establishment period. Where agricultural land was retained in local authority ownership it was usually occupied by farmers on short term grazing licences. Under the terms of such licences the landowner is normally responsible for maintenance operations such as fertilising and repairing of fences or hedges. In general it was apparent that licensees undertook a greater proportion of the maintenance of the land than would normally be expected under such agreements. However, there was a natural reluctance on the part of licensees to put too much into the land unless confident that the licence would be renewed in subsequent years.

The level of maintenance of recreation areas (mostly winter pitches) was generally lower than considered appropriate to provide a reasonable quality pitch capable of sustaining weekly use. This was due to less frequent cutting than would be expected together with lack of fertilising, weed control and other maintenance inputs.

In most cases there were only small differences between annual costs of maintenance during the establishment period and the subsequent long term annual costs. This does not apply to tree and shrub management where the intial maintenance required is much higher than that required after establishment. The local authorities' costs of maintaining plantings during establishment were similar to those required by the model.

However the balance of effort was more towards replacing trees which had failed than encouraging the successful establishment of planted stock. Replanting was often carried out to replace trees destroyed by vandalism. This was usually necessary only where standard trees were planted at low density. Mass planting of smaller stock is less susceptible to vandalism. Fertilising and weed control inputs were in general lower than required for successful establishment and this was reflected in the condition of many plantings.

8.2 Cost Effective Land Management Strategies

The cost effectiveness of land management strategies for the various categories of afteruse of sites are considered in turn below. For each afteruse current practice is discussed together with consideration of:

— the management strategies available for each afteruse and under what circumstances they are applicable;

— factors to be taken into account in design of schemes in order to minimise management costs;

— the income and expenditure which should be budgeted for.

8.2.1 Public Open Space

All the open space sites were in local authority ownership and this will normally be the most appropriate option. Where sites are reclaimed for housing it may be possible to vest ownership of associated open space areas in residents associations or similar organisations who would then have direct responsibility for maintenance. The legal and administrative implications of such arrangements would require careful investigation.

The main choice of maintenance strategy for public open space areas is between the 'naturalistic' approach based on ecological principles of design and maintenance and the 'traditional' approach of mown grass with standard trees. Both approaches have their advantages and disadvantages. Sites restored using a 'naturalistic' approach can be visually attractive with relatively low maintenance costs, in urban areas they provide opportunities for experiencing and understanding the natural environment and they provide habitats for wildlife. Among the disadvantages of such schemes may be the need for careful control of maintenance and the possible dangers of providing cover for the antisocial elements of society. Sites restored on traditional lines if well maintained can have high visual impact and appear well cared for. The main disadvantage is the high maintenance costs needed for upkeep to a high standard.

Both strategies have their place on reclaimed derelict sites. The main factor influencing the choice of strategy is the level and pattern of use of sites. Where reclaimed sites are in prominent positions in urban areas or are subject to heavy use then the traditional approach is most applicable. Sites which are less subject to pressure of use and which are not prominent in urban situations or are in urban fringe or rural locations provide opportunities for the naturalistic approach. On large sites there are opportunities for a combination of strategies in a zonal approach. Such an approach with three zones has been well summarized by Corder (1986) as follows:

"

Zone 1 Traditional planting and management techniques in the immediate vicinity of intense human activity or interest e.g. civic areas, adjacent to pedestrian/vehicular routes, features/paths in urban parks and around residential areas.

Zone 2 An intermediate zone, less subject to human involvement and one in which a certain incursion of natural plant associations and reduced management levels would be acceptable. Golf courses are an existing example and many areas in public parks and school grounds have potential.

Zone 3 Peripheral areas in which rich natural communities could be created and appropriately managed. Steep embankments in school grounds are an obvious example as are the numerous out-of-the-way corners, so often neglected, evident in urban areas. "

Maintenance of all sites in the study was carried out by direct labour organisations of local authorities, normally part of Leisure and Amenities or equivalent departments. Under the compulsory competitive tendering requirements of the Local Government Act 1988 the use of outside contractors may increase but the extent to which they will be able to compete effectively with local authority direct labour cannot be predicted at present.

In many cases local authorities' awareness of the costs of maintaining individual sites was poor since maintenance programmes were costed over all open space in their control. It is essential that information on maintenance is available on a site specific basis if land managers are to make informed decisions regarding maintenance programmes. The need to draw up detailed work schedules for tendering and contracting purposes should improve the current poor situation. Local authorities were engaged in quantifying maintenance inputs to sites at the time of the survey. From our enquiries it was apparent that this exercise was concentrating on quantifying the maintenance currently carried out on sites so that tenders could be invited on that basis. The opportunity which this exercise presents for considering alternative management strategies was not being taken.

Maintenance costs can be reduced by careful consideration at the design stage. For example areas of mown grass should be designed so that edges along footpaths and other hard landscape features can be cut easily with the same machine used on the remainder of the area. Footpaths in general should coincide with desire lines and may be constructed after these have been established by use. More informal footpaths may be created cheaply and effectively by mowing swathes through paddock length or long grass. Reducing the frequency of mowing of grassland will substantially reduce overall costs. Frequent mowing should be restricted as far as possible to areas of intensive use within sites. There are some organizational problems which must be overcome in order to achieve this. Increasing the proportion of sites planted to trees and shrubs also reduces the long term costs of maintenance. This is discussed more fully in Section 8.2.3 below.

Among the sites which were most successful were those which provided for a range of activities and incorporated features such as children's playgrounds, kickabout areas and cycle tracks. Several successful sites formed integral parts of larger areas of open space. In some cases local groups took a direct interest in sites. This helped to maximise the benefits derived from the sites and reduced vandalism. Vandalism, particularly to trees and fences, was a considerable problem on small urban sites.

One particular group who are poorly catered for at present are young motorcyclists. Unofficial use of several sites by trail bikes was resulting in problems. There are difficulties in providing suitable areas for this purpose since it does not readily mix with other uses and there are legal problems relating to liability for accidents.

It is essential that maintenance requirements of sites are fully considered at the design stage. Although some local authorities did consider this in some detail, in many instances this was not the case and although the need for expenditure on maintenance was recognised detailed costings were not prepared.

A budget price of approximately £1,000/ha/annum should be allowed for maintenance of small urban public open space sites involving use of pedestrian machines for cutting grass. Costs are reduced as the size of site increases to around £200/ha/annum for sites of more than 3 ha or so. When a purely naturalistic approach is adopted maintenance costs in the range of £100–200/ha/annum would be expected.

8.2.2 Agriculture

Agricultural afteruses of reclaimed derelict sites should be seen as a management tool which serves to maintain the land in an acceptable physical and visual condition while minimising local authorities' maintenance costs. Agriculture is only a practical option on those rural or urban fringe sites which are sufficiently large and suitably placed to enable effective management by a local farmer to be a practical proposition. Several strategies regarding tenure of agricultural land are available to local authorities as described in section 3.6.2. The amount of control by the local authority varies from the high degree afforded by short term grazing licences to the low degree if land is tenanted or sold. In general where sites have been restored with shallow soil cover over poor materials where regression may occur, then it is preferable for land to be let on short term licences so that remedial action can be taken in good time. If, however, restoration is to a high quality and there is no reason to expect later regression then tenancy or sale of the land may be a better option since it gives the occupier a long term interset in the maintenance of quality of the site. Tenants and licensees should be given advice on crop and soil management particularly in the early years after reclamation.

The majority of agricultural sites included in the study were in local authority ownership and let on short term licences. A few sites were tenanted or sold. There are advantages in short term letting of land in that the maintenance of the land should remain under the direct control of the local authority. However, in practice maintenance of sites was often left almost entirely to licensees. Since they have no long term interest in the land they are reluctant to invest much effort in maintenance operations. Indeed under the terms of licence agreements such investments should not be permitted since, if the land is occupied by the same person year after year and that person performs operations that improve the land, he may be held to have established a full tenancy. It was apparent that the arrangements under which land was occupied and the responsibilities of landlords (in this case local authorities) and occupiers were unclear in many cases.

Local authorities in general have misgivings regarding the sale of sites since they would then lose control over managment. There are concerns over the possibility of regression of sites and the problems which this might cause should the land have been sold.

In the design of agricultural restoration it is important to provide for flexibility of operations so that the land can be easily accommodated into the farm unit. Otherwise the land will become a liability, maintenance will be neglected and the site will decline. In order to be flexible in agricultural terms land must be well drained, necessitating adequate but not extreme gradients and possibly underdrainage. Access must be good and a water supply available for stock grazing. Adequate fencing must be provided and maintained at grazed sites.

The appropriate cropping for most sites is some form of grassland, particularly when restoration requires that soils be imported. This in any event reflected the predominant agricultural land use in the vicinity of many sites. There are a number of options for management of grassland ranging from low input, low output extensive grazing to high input, high output silage production. All may be appropriate on reclaimed derelict sites. The low input options are particularly suited to nature conservation sites where they help to promote a diverse flora. High input systems are suited to lowland sites with a good depth of soil capable of sustaining intensive cropping.

There are few occasions where arable cropping would be appropriate, particulary in view of the high cost of importing a sufficient depth of soil for successful arable cropping. The only crops which could be realistically grown would be the less demanding crops such as cereals and possible oilseed rape. At a time when farmers are being paid to take land out of cereal production under the set-aside scheme the creation of further cereal growing land at high cost is not an effective strategy. Difficulties may arise where sites are restored to agriculture adjacent to housing areas. Utilisation of the land may be limited and grazing prevented by the problems of interference with stock. In such cases restoration to arable use may be preferable in agricultural terms, but agriculture may not be the most appropriate use in such cases and alternative afteruses should be considered. Horse grazing may be one option on some urban fringe sites but can present management difficulties (Section 5.2.1).

Where land is licenced the local authority budget for maintenance at a moderate input level should be of the order of £200/ha/annum. Income of £150-200/ha/annum should be obtainable for grazing licences but this will depend on the local agricultural economy and lower fees may have to be accepted in order to ensure that maintenance of the land continues. In practice fees from licencing were in general not sufficient to cover the total costs of administering and maintaining the land.

8.2.3 Woodland

Woodland sites were all in local authority ownership, in the majority of cases county councils. Woodlands are of great importance in the landscape and as amenity areas and it is desirable that local authorities should in general retain control of their management.

Most county councils have forestry teams who carry out maintenance. District councils have some capabilities but often use contractors under the direction of a tree or woodland officer. Under the requirements for compulsory competitive tendering it is possible that the use of contractors may increase. It is important that the specialist capability for specifying and supervising contracts remains within local authorities.

The objectives of woodland plantings must be established from the outset. The main management strategies for woodland are commercial timber production or amenity/wildlife promotion. Where large areas of 5 ha or so of relatively even ground are available, then planting for commercial objectives may be feasible. However in most cases the visual, amenity and nature conservation characteristics of plantings are of greater significance and should be given priority in planting design and species selection. Several examples of uses of inappropriate species were seen during the survey resulting in failure. It is important that the species selected for planting should suit the site conditions.

In order to reduce maintenance costs it is important that good vehicle access is provided to all areas of site. This is particularly important for weed control which may involve large volumes of water for sprays. Use of fast growing, rapidly establishing species will reduce the length of the period over which weed control is required and hence the costs.

In general ground preparation and tree planting are standard operations easily specified in contract documents although there are particular problems associated with some materials which require specialist techniques. Proper handling and planting techniques, specification of quality of plants and protection against damage by animals will help to minimise losses during establishment. However early maintenance of trees is of equal importance to good establishment and in many cases was not carried out effectively. Weed control was often given poor attention. Tree seeding techniques may have potential on derelict sites but methods are at a relatively early stage of development and practical experience is limited.

There was tendency to beat up plantations thoughtlessly with little consideration of the reasons for initial failure. Where a particular area of a site is clearly not going to support trees, then this effort is wasted. In some cases it should be possible to predict such areas and design plantings accordingly. For example the exposed tops of draughty spoil heaps were often areas where tree plantings had failed. Some local authorities did not beat up plantings leaving the open areas resulting from failures as glades in the developing woodland. Providing failures are not excessive this is a good strategy which adds to the diversity, conservation and amenity value of the site.

Local authority budgets for woodland maintenance should be of the order of £300-400/ha/annum during the four or five year establishment phase, falling to around £80-140/ha/annum once well established. There are opportunities for income from woodland from thinnings and harvesting of timber. The relatively recent dates of the reclamation schemes included in the survey prevented an assessment of the potential incomes which could be derived but this deserves investigation.

8.2.4 Nature Conservation

There are two main nature conservation strategies which may be relevant on reclaimed derelict sites. The first is nature conservation in the strict sense where the priority is the protection and conservation of wildlife. The second is conservation of wildlife as an amenity and educational resource. Nature conservation in the strict sense will only normally be appropriate where sites have been naturally colonised by vegetation of high conservation value. There are many examples of such sites. Some of these, including some lime waste tips and quarries, are statutory Sites of Special Scientific Interest. The conservation of wildlife for its amenity and educational value may be appropriate on a much wider range of sites and habitats may be specifically designed and constructed for this purpose. These strategies need not be mutually exclusive and zoning within sites is usually possible. Nature conservation can be integrated into other land uses, particularly public open space (overlapping with the 'naturalistic' approach to open space) and woodland and may form part of mixed end use sites for example with agricultural restoration.

In order to avoid excessively complex and possibly costly maintenance inputs it is not good policy to attempt to produce too complex a mix of habitats within a site. A few habitats providing a range of structural elements such as grassland, scrub and woodland will be of more value than, for example, a complex mixture of grass communities.

The number of sites restored specifically for nature conservation included in the survey was small. However several sites in the public open space, woodland and mixed after use categories included areas of nature conservation interest. Ownership of these sites generally lies with local authorities. In some cases they were leased to local naturalists' trusts. One site was owned by a trust. Because of their limited resources and particular priorities local trusts tended to be only interested in sites with an existing high nature conservation value and not with those with potential for development of such interest. It is thus difficult to interest these organisation in many restored sites. Where sites are directly managed by local authorities it is important that there is a commitment to manage for conservation if sites are to be successful and not degrade into wilderness. The employment of wardens/rangers was seen to be particularly effective. In addition to carrying out and supervising maintenance work they had several other important functions including deterring vandalism, encouraging volunteers to assist in maintenance operations, interpreting the site to visitors and an important educational role in guiding school parties around sites and visiting schools to talk to classes. If sensitively managed nature conservation sites have wider benefits for recreation, amenity and education than is often recognised. This is particularly so when a warden/ranger is present. Such a service can cover a number of small sites and need not be restricted to those covering large areas.

It is important that detailed management plans are prepared for these sites and that nature conservation is not considered as a no managment option. However the nature conservation value of sites will usually be enhanced under low input systems and will be relatively inexpensive. The nature conservation value of a site is to a great extent dependent on diversity of habitats present and thus variation in soils, topography and vegetation types is beneficial. Incorporation of existing vegetation in reclamation schemes is sometimes possible adding considerably to the interest of sites. The potential for linking features within sites to existing wildlife habitats outside sites should be explored where opportunities arise.

It is often possible to encourage local volunteers to undertake maintenance operations which would be beyond the resources of the local authority. At sites included in the survey this included footpath construction, tree planting and thinning and coppicing of woodlands. It is important that the efforts of volunteers are well supervised to ensure that they are effective.

It is very difficult to give budget figures for maintenance of conservation areas since the cost of maintaining particular vegetation types varies widely, and only a small number of sites were available for our study. However, in most cases vegetation managed for nature conservation will require lower inputs than vegetation managed for more intensive uses.

There are opportunities for deriving income from nature conservation sites from fishing, grazing rents, sale of hay, woodland products such as thinnings and coppice poles and sale of interpretive material. This potential was realised to some extent at the sites studied.

8.2.5 Recreation

All the recreation sites included in the survey were in local authority ownership, usually district councils. Most were winter pitches. There may be opportunities to rent pitches to local clubs but this was not common. All sites were maintained by local authority staff. The use of contractors may increase under the requirements for compulsory competitive tendering.

The main strategies for recreation sites are to provide either a high performance facility which is capable of sustaining a high degree of wear and use, or one of low performance which does not stand a high level of use. In practice the latter strategy was most commonly adopted on sites visited.

In many cases levels of maintenance were insufficient to maintain pitches to a reasonable standard. At some sites maintenance did not differ from that of informal open space resulting in poor pitch conditions. This is not necessarily the most cost effective strategy since opportunities for deriving income are missed.

Where land is to be restored to sports pitches then particular attention must be paid to gradients, soil texture and especially drainage. This results in high capital costs which were not all eligible for Derelict Land Grant. Finance may be available from other sources such as the Sports Council. If these investments are to be worthwhile then there must be an identified need for the facility and a commitment to the high maintenance inputs which will be required.

In order to maintain pitches to a reasonable standard, maintenance budgets of around £1,000/ha/annum should be allowed. There may be opportunities for income from pitch fees from well maintained pitches but in general these were not realised.

8.2.6 Mixed Use Sites

Strategies for the individual elements of mixed after use sites are discussed above. It is important that management of the various components of sites is coordinated and that there is effective liaison between the various organisations which may be involved. A number of sites studied showed successful integration of afteruses, the most common combinations being agriculture and woodland and public open space and woodland. The inclusion of agricultural land in mixed end use schemes is beneficial in that where sufficient income is generated this may be used to offset the costs of maintenance of other land.

8.3 Captial and Maintenance Costs and Performance of Sites

The relationships between capital costs of reclamation and subsequent maintenance costs on the performance of sites are discussed in Section 7.0 of this report.

Restoration to nature conservation was found to be a highly cost effective option where low captial costs as a result of use of pre-existing vegetation as far as possible were associated with low maintenance costs, and relatively high levels of benefits. These benefits were not only for nature conservation but also encompassed organised and informal recreation, education and visual amenity. The low cost approach used on such sites could be applied to many sites where nature conservation per se is not the intended afteruse. There are many sites where vegetation has naturally colonised a significant area and suitable low cost treatment would be feasible.

A recent survey of derelict land in Wales showed that more than half the sites studied had an average plant cover of greater than 30% indicating that many sites would be suitable for such treatments (W.D.A. 1987).

The traditional public open spaces of mown grass with standard trees, particularly small urban sites were expensive to reclaim and to maintain. Performance measured in this study was relatively low although some were of considerable benefit in their immediate locality. Larger sites were more cost effective with lower capital and maintenance costs as a result of economies of scale. However at some sites there was scope for reduction in maintenance costs by more sensitive land management. Reduction of mowing frequencies in grassland areas would produce the most immediate cost reduction. Planting more land with woodland blocks increases captial costs but maintenance requirements would be reduced. Woodland blocks have high amenity, visual and nature conservation values. As discussed in section 5.4, woodland sites have high planting and establishment costs but low costs of maintenance once the canopies of young trees have closed, shading out competitive weed growth. In addition the potential income from thinning (although small) and felling will help to offset the initial high costs. The long term economics of woodland management on derelict sites over the complete planting and harvesting cycles were beyond the scope of this project. With increasing interest in 'urban forestry' this is a subject which merits investigation.

The high capital and maintenance costs of recreation areas can only be justified where there is an identified need for the facility and a commitment to carry out maintenance at an appropriate level. Income from facilities should be obtainable to offset these costs although it is unlikely that they could be fully covered.

Restoration to agricultural use was the only land use option where zero net costs of maintenance to local authorities should be readily achieveable. In fact it may be possible for local authorities to derive a net income from these sites. However, on the sites discussed, most of which were let on short term grazing licences, the income derived from the land was generally insufficient to cover the maintenance and management requirements. In most cases licensees were in fact providing a higher level of management input than would normally be expected. As discussed in Section 8.2, letting of land under tenancies should encourage a higher quality of management than is the case at present while retaining a certain amount of control with the local authority. The performance of agricultural sites as assessed in Section 6.0 is relatively low since the main benefits largely accrue to the licensees in terms of crops and livestock production and sites were of little value for factors such as amenity and nature conservation.

9. Summary and Recommendations

This report describes research carried out for the Department of the Environment investigating the cost effectiveness of management of sites reclaimed to 'soft' end uses under the Derelict Land Grant Scheme. The end uses considered were public open space, agriculture, recreation, woodland, nature conservation and mixed sites containing two or more of these uses.

The main objectives of the research were to:

(i) identify cost effective strategies for the management of reclaimed derelict sites;

(ii) assess the extent to which these management strategies are affected by the methods and costs of the initial reclamation.

In order to achieve these objectives details of a representative sample of projects completed between 1978 and 1984 were obtained from the D.o.E. and local authority sources, and from site visits. The information sought included details of the pre-reclamation condition of the sites, site investigation and reclamation work carried out and subsequent management and maintenance. Information on costs was sought where relevant. While detailed costs of reclamation could be obtained for a high proportion of sites, information on management and maintenance costs was limited and highly variable. Some authorities did not have data available on these costs and others were unable to give a breakdown on a site basis. Where costs could be identified they were highly site specific and depended on site conditions, location, access and size, organisation of labour and machinery used. Standard costs for typical maintenance operations were derived from a range of published and unpublished sources together with information provided by local authorities. Maintenance models were derived for sites based on ground cover present, the maintainance requirements of the ground cover and standard costs. The limitations of this system must be appreciated in interpreting the results of the work. The costs of site maintenance derived are intended as general guides to typical costs for particular operations, ground covers and sites and not as accurate site specific costings. The present use and performance of sites was assessed and compared with capital and maintenance costs in order to assess cost effectiveness.

In examining the full range of 'soft' end uses the number of sites in any particular category was low. This again imposes restrictions on the interpretation of the data, particularly in the case of nature conservation sites.

This section of the report summarises the main findings and conclusions of the project. Recommendations arising from the research are included and set out in bold type.

9.1 Restoration Problems and Solutions

Derelict sites presented physical and chemical problems affecting reclamation as described in Section 3.3. The main physical problems were those associated with underground structures such as foundations and mine shafts and those resulting from the nature of materials on site including stability, soil texture and structure and water holding characteristics. The main chemical problems were deficiencies of plant nutrients, the problems of high or low pH and the presence of toxic chemicals.

The nature of pre-reclamation site investigations varied between types of site (Section 3.2). In some cases the need for a particular type of survey was related to the afteruse of the site (e.g. level surveys, drainage surveys, soil surveys and soil nutrient status). In other cases the need was more closley related to the previous use of the site (e.g. contamination, underground structures, stability and combustibility).

Pre-reclamation surveys of sites should be comprehensive, multi-disciplinary in approach and fully recorded (see Appendix 1).

In some cases there were associations between types of dereliction and the afteruse of sites (Section 3.1). For example former housing sites were normally restored to public open space while the afteruse of colliery spoil heaps was normally agriculture, woodland or mixed end uses. This reflected the location and size of sites rather than their intrinsic characteristics.

The choice of afteruses for reclaimed derelict sites should be based on need and demand followed by

careful consideration of site characteristics and the requirements of afteruses.

The planning and design of reclamation schemes was carried out almost exclusively by local authority staff (Section 3.4.1). The framework within which staff involved in reclamation operated varied widely between authorities.

Design of schemes must involve inputs from a range of disciplines including engineers, landscape architects and land managers.

The methods used in reclamation of sites ranged from minimal treatments utilising existing vegetation to major earthmoving and regrading, importing of soils and establishment of vegetation in this newly placed material (see Section 3.4)

Restoration should make use of existing features particularly vegetation on sites wherever possible.

In design of revegetation/planting for derelict sites, species selection should take account of site conditions. For example use of a few resilient tree species which will thrive is preferable to complex mixed species plantings, a large proportion of which may fail. Underplanting or replacement with a wider range of species can be carried out later when site conditions have improved. Current practice is often to view the initial planting as the 'end product' since the work under DLG is seen as the only opportunity for extensive planting. There is a need for a more flexible and long term approach to planting design.

It is important that land is restored to a quality which is appropriate to its intended use. If restoration is to a lower quality, then the site may not be used to its full potential.

The relationship of restored sites to adjoining land uses was examined and found to vary between the various types of site (Section 3.5). Use of agricultural sites was most closely related to surrounding land use while woodland was least closely related. Sites also varied with respect to the extent of which they were affected by public pressure. Small public open space sites were subject to a high degree of public pressure while agriculture and nature conservation sites were little affected. This was largely related to the location of sites with respect to urban, urban fringe and rural settings.

The need for flexibility in design of schemes should be taken into account, particularly in urban fringe areas where the land uses in the area surrounding the site are liable to change.

Almost all the sites remained in local authority ownership after reclamation and most were directly maintained by local authorities (Section 3.6). The main exception was agricultural land where most was let on annual grazing or mowing licences.

9.2 Reclamation Costs

Costs of reclamation were converted to 1986/87 prices so that comparisons could be made (Section 2.5). Costs were highly variable and site specific and few statistically significant differences between costs for the various afteruse categories could be identified but trends were evident (Section 4.0). Size of site was an important determinant of the cost of reclamation to public open space, small sites being particularly costly (Section 4.5). Restoration to recreation was also relatively expensive. Restoration to nature conservation was least costly. For the majority of sites no significant funding other than Derelict Land Grant was used to finance reclamation (Section 4.6).

It is essential that full records of costs and methods of reclamation are kept. If this is not done the vast body of experience of derelict land reclamation cannot be made available for future reference.

9.3 Management and Maintenance

In the context of this report 'management' refers to the control and administration of the various afteruses, whilst 'maintenance' describes the operations carried out.

The organisation of management and maintenance varied between local authorities (Section 5.1). In general responsibility for management within county councils lay with a technical services department whilst maintenance was carried out either by a direct labour organisation or outside contractor. Within district councils management responsibility was usually passed to a leisure services or similar department who also carried out maintenance using direct labour. Some limited information on administration costs was obtained but these were broad estimates only and varied widely between sites. The data suggested that costs were comparable with published information suggesting that 55% of expenditure may be attributed to management costs and 45% to maintenance and repairs.

Although the potential for generating income applies to all afteruses to some degree with the exception of small public open space sites (Section 5.1.4), agriculture was the only afteruse which produced income to a significant extent. The average annual income including licenced and tenanted land was £130/ha.

Where the possibility of deriving income from sites exists, this should be investigated. If additional capital

or revenue costs will be incurred in realising this income, then these must be considered in relation to the benefits which will be derived.

Maintenance of sites is described in the report with respect to the main types of ground cover present on sites. These were agricultural grassland, amenity grassland and trees and shrubs. Information on maintenance carried out and its costs were obtained from local authorities were available. Maintenance models for each ground cover were derived and costed using standard costs. The model costs were compared with local authority costs where these were available.

The annual model maintenance costs for agricultural grassland were £147/ha, £216/ha and £319/ha for low, medium and high input systems respectively (Section 5.2.5). The average local authority cost was £124/ha. The figures suggested that the local authorities adopted a low input strategy. In some cases this was appropriate but for the majority of sites maintenance more in line with the moderate input model would be more suitable. No information on harvesting costs or yields was available. Rents were generally sufficient to cover maintenace costs but not to cover all management costs if administration expenses were taken into account.

Model annual maintenance costs for amenity grassland were derived for a range of mowing regimes and area mown (Section 5.3.4). Costs varied from £105/ha for 'paddock' length areas larger than 5 ha to £1,015/ha for close mown areas smaller than 0.5 ha. Local authority costs were comparable with the models. The annual model maintenance costs derived for sports pitches was £1,040/ha. Local authority inputs were generally at a lower level (Section 5.3.5).

In the case of woodland model maintenance costs derived for the 'establishment' period (i.e. years 2–5 after planting) were £373/ha for plantings of less than 1 ha and £323/ha for larger plantings. Annual model maintenance costs after the 'establishment' period were £138/ha and £88/ha respectively (Section 5.4.4). Comparison with local authority costs and operations suggested that considerable maintenance was being carried out but funds were directed more towards replacement of failures than encouraging the establishment and growth of the initial planting.

In design of reclamation schemes the maintenance costs, both in the short and long term should be set out in detail. It is essential that managment and maintenance is fully costed on a site basis since it is difficult to make informed decisions aimed at increasing cost effectiveness without this information. A commitment to fund the management of the land needs to be made at the design stage.

Management plans should be prepared for all sites. Sites should be monitored and plans should be regularly reviewed, we suggest at five year intervals, and programmes revised where necessary.

In preparing detailed work schedules for sites for tendering and contracting purposes, the maintenance requirements should be reviewed and inputs adjusted as necessary.

9.4 Present Use and Performance of Sites

The present use and performance of sites was assessed largely on the basis of observations made on site visits. Use and performance were assessed under the five main criteria of:

(i) Safety

(ii) Land Use Compatibility

(iii) Visual Benefit

(iv) Amenity Use

(v) Nature Conservation Value

A numerical scoring system was used which provided a systematic and standard procedure for ranking sites in terms of use and performance, in spite of disadvantages arising from: interdependence of criteria; to some extent its arbitrary and subjective nature; and difficulty in scoring some criteria and values.

The afteruse categories with the highest average overall score for use and performance were public open space sites above 5 ha in size. These sites tended to be of high visual benefit and scored highly for amenity use and nature conservation value (section 6.3.6). The lowest score was that for temporary public open space. Agricultural sites also had a low average score as a result of low amenity use and nature conservation values. Recreation and small public open space sites also had low overall average scores with particularly low scores for nature conservation value.

In addition to the five main criteria other factors were also assessed during visits (section 6.4). These were:

(i) Site Maintenance

(ii) Public Pressure

(iii) Physical and Chemical Factors

(iv) Vegetation Quality

These factors did not contribute to the overall scores for sites.

9.5 Cost Effectiveness

Cost effectiveness may be defined as the achievement of strategic objectives within a generally acceptable level of expenditure. In assessing cost effectiveness the costs of carrying out reclamation and maintaining sites and the benefits arising from the restored land were taken into account. The relationships between capital costs and performance; maintenance costs and performance; and capital and maintenance costs were considered.

In comparing capital costs with performance wide variations between the afteruse categories were found (Section 7.1). The most cost effective sites in these terms were those restored to nature conservation where low capital costs were associated with high overall benefits. Large public open space sites were also realtively cost effective as a result of the economies of scale associated with reclaiming large areas and the high visual and amenity benefits provided by these sites. Woodland sites were relatively cost effective due to the low capital costs of reclamation. The least cost effective afteruse categories in terms of the relationship between capital costs and performance were public open space sites of less than 0.5 ha, temporary public open space and recreation sites.

In comparing maintenance costs with performance no direct relationship between the level of maintenance and the performance of sites was found (Section 7.2). However there was a direct relationship between the effectiveness of site maintenance and the extent to which the local authority maintenance inputs accorded with those derived from the model maintenance programmes.

When capital and maintenance costs were compared it was found that in geneeral they were directly related (Section 7.3). It is likely that factors such as size of site and ease of access affect both the reclamation and maintenance costs.

9.6 Conclusions

The report concludes with a discussion of the findings of the research under three main headings of:

1. Annual maintenance costs and operations

2. Cost effective land management strategies

3. Captial and maintenance costs and performance of sites

9.6.1. Annual Maintenance Costs and Operations

The annual maintenance costs and operations carried out by local authorities were generally found to be comparable with the models for particular ground cover types with some exceptions (Section 8.1). Maintenance of agricultural land tended to be at a low level, particularly after the establishment period and it was apparent that licensees undertook a greater proportion of maintenance than would normally be expected. The level of maintenance of recreation areas (mostly winter pitches) was generally lower than considered appropriate to provide a reasonable quality pitch. In most cases there were only small differences between annual maintenance costs during the 'establishment' period and the subsequent long term maintenance costs. This did not apply to tree and shrub plantings where initial maintenance requirements were much greater than long term costs. It was apparent that local authorities concentrated their efforts more on replacing failed trees than encouraging the successful establishment of planted stock.

9.6.2 Cost Effective Land Management Strategies

The cost effectiveness of land management strategies for each afteruse was discussed in terms of:

— the management strategies available for each afteruse and under what circumstances they are applicable;

— factors to be taken into account in design of schemes in order to minimise management costs;

— the income and expenditure which should be budgeted for.

9.6.2.1 Public Open Space The main choice of management strategy for public open space is between the 'naturalistic' approach based on ecological principles of design and maintenance and the 'traditional' approach of mown grass with standard trees (Section 8.2.1). Both strategies have their place on reclaimed derelict sites, the main factor influencing choice being the level and pattern of use of sites. Maintenance costs can be reduced by careful consideration and attention to detail at the design stage, particularly with reference to treatment of edges, choice of mowing regimes and proportion of sites which can be planted with trees and shrubs. An annual budget of approximately £1,000/ha should be allowed for maintenance for small 'traditional' public open space sites. Costs are reduced as the size of site increases to around £200/ha for sites of more than 3 ha or so. Where a naturalistic approach is adopted maintenance costs in the range of £100–200/ha would be expected.

Derelict sites in urban settings and larger sites in urban fringe and rural locations are appropriate for reclamation to public open space. The priority for reclamation schemes for small urban sites should be to provide informal amenity areas for the inhabitants of

the immediate neighbourhood. Larger more rural sites should be developed in a country park style with the needs of more mobile sectors of a wider population in mind.

Vegetation cover should be designed so as to reduce long term maintenance costs. Increasing areas of tree and shrub planting, and reducing frequency of grass cutting are effective means of reducing maintenance costs. Block planting of trees and shrubs is preferable to use of standards.

A 'naturalistic' landscape approach should be adopted where possible. Such an approach based on ecological principles of revegetation and maintenance will produce a result which is cheaper to maintain than traditional open space areas. The result is robust and capable of withstanding public pressure, vandalism and play.

Provisions for a range of activities should be made where possible to encourage use of sites e.g. children's play facilities, kickabout areas, cycle tracks, trim tracks. Most such facilities are not eligible for DLG.

Maintenance programmes and costs should be regularly reviewed and revised where necessary. This applies particularly to grass cutting where options for varying regimes on different parts of sites should be taken.

Where sites are restored to temporary open space pending future development schemes, use should made of low cost methods of establishing and maintaining grass swards without the use of topsoil.

9.6.2.2 Agriculture Agriculture as an afteruse of reclaimed derelict sites should be seen as a management tool which serves to maintain the land in an acceptable condition while minimising local authorities' maintenance costs (Section 8.2.2). In general where sites have been restored with shallow soil cover over poor materials then it is preferable for land to be let on short term licences so that remedial action can be taken in good time where necessary. If restoration is to a high quality and there is no reason to expect later regression then tenancy or sale of land may be a better option. The appropriate cropping for most sites is grassland. There are a number of options for management ranging from low input/low output extensive grazing to high input/high output silage production all of which may be appropriate to particular sites. Where land is licenced the local authority annual budget for maintenance at a moderate input level should be approximately £200/ha. Income of £150–200/ha should be obtainable from grazing licences but this will depend on the local agricultural economy. Lower fees may have to be accepted to ensure that maintenance of the land continues.

Agriculture in the context of derelict land reclamation and afteruse should be seen as a management tool rather than an end use for its own sake. Sites should only be restored to agriculture where the means to effectively farm the land can be identified. Rents/ licence fees should be set at a level which the local agricultural economy permits to ensure continued use of the land.

It is essential that the terms of the agreements under which land may be occupied are properly defined and fulfilled otherwise there is a risk of establishing full tenancies.

Except for very low rates of stocking used to maintain visual appearance, topsoil depths exceeding the 150 mm eligible for DLG will be needed unless the substrate is unusually favourable. The soil depth required should be determined for each individual site taking into account the agricultural afteruse intended, the nature of topsoil, subsoil and substrate materials available, and the requirements for underdrainage and secondary treatments. A safe margin of error should be allowed to accommodate variations in depth over the site.

Management of sites should include regular monitoring of nutrient status to guide fertilizer inputs. Monitoring of toxicity should also be carried out where relevant.

In many cases it would be preferable for sites to be let on short term agreements following reclamation. Only when local authorities are happy that sites are fully established and that occupiers can manage sites competently should full tenancies or sale of land be considered.

9.6.2.3 Woodland The main priorities of woodland planting on reclaimed derelict sites were visual, amenity and nature conservation (Section 8.2.3). It is important that species selection and design of plantings take account of site conditions and that good access is provided for maintenance. Early maintenance of planting, particularly weed control was often neglected. Local authority annual budgets for woodland maintenance should be of the order of £300–400/ha during the four or five year establishment phase and approximately £80 – 140/ha once well established. Assessment of the potential income which could be derived from plantings was beyond the scope of this study but deserves further investigation.

The responsibility for management of woodland areas should remain with local authorities and a specialist capability for supervising maintenance retained.

In design and maintenance of planting schemes on derelict sites the visual amenity and nature conservation aspects will normally be more important

than commercial objectives. Opportunities for deriving income should however be explored whenever possible.

Selection of species appropriate to site conditions is essential to the success of a planting scheme. Plantings on poor soil should normally include a high proportion of fast growing resilient species such as Common and Grey alder, Grey poplar, Goat willow and Rowan which thrive under a wide range of conditions.

Planting schemes should take into account variations within sites particularly of soil and drainage characteristics.

More attention should be given to careful site preparation, planting and care of young trees (particularly weed control) than is often the case.

The long term economics of woodlands on derelict sites and in urban areas generally should be investigated.

9.6.2.4 Nature Conservation There are two main nature conservation strategies which may be relevant on reclaimed on derelict sites (Section 8.2.4). Firstly, nature conservation in the strict sense where the priority is the protection and conservation of wildlife, and secondly conservation of wildlife as an amenity and educational resource. Nature conservation in the strict sense may be appropriate where sites have been naturally colonised by vegetation of high conservation value. Conservation of wildlife for its amenity and educational value is approrpriate on a much wider range of sites. These strategies are not mutually exclusive and nature conservation can be integrated into other land uses. Nature conservation is not a 'no-management' option and detailed management plans should be prepared for sites. The employment of wardens/rangers was seen to be particularly effective in maintaining sites and encouraging and supervising their use. It is often possible to involve volunteers in site maintenance.

Derelict land provides opportunities for conservation and creation of 'restored' habitats as an amenity/ educational resource, and also for nature conservation in the stricter sense of conserving and maintaining species and habitats. Both these aspects should be recognized in design of reclamation schemes.

There are opportunities for intergrating elements of nature conservation interest into many sites where other land uses are dominant e.g. public open space, woodland and agriculture. Such opportunities should be taken wherever possible.

Nature conservation as an end use in itself should only be adopted where site conditions are appropriate. In general nutrient poor soils and retention of existing and adjoining vegetation are the key elements in successful restoration to nature conservation. Sites providing a range of drainage conditions can also be particularly suitable for a nature conservation afteruse.

Site surveys assume particular importance where nature conservation is proposed. Such surveys will identify areas of existing vegetation which can be retained, and indicte the capability of substrates to support vegetation, and appropriate species for planting and seeding.

The low nutrient, low competition characteristics of some waste materials can result in a vegetation of high conservation interest in a local and sometimes national context. This should be taken into account in site assessment and design.

Nature conservation must not be seen as a 'zero maintenance' option. If sites are to succeed maintenance programmes must be defined and reviewed as for any other afteruse.

The opportunities for recreation, amenity and educational uses of nature conservation areas should be fully addressed.

The employment of wardens/rangers to manage and maintain nature conservation sites results in effective use of sites and is to be recommended.

When volunteers are used to carry out maintenance on sites they must be well supervised.

Low input agriculture may be an appropriate management option on suitable sites.

9.6.2.5 Recreation Most recreation sites included in the study were winter pitches (Section 8.2.5). In many cases the restoration and maintenance were of insufficient quality to provide pitches of a reasonable standard. Where land is to be restored to sports pitches then the high quality of restoration required is not all eligible for Derelict Land Grant. If the high investments are to be worthwhile there must be an identified need for the facility and a commitment to the high annual maintenance inputs of approximately £1,000/ha required.

The maintenance requirements of pitches are higher than for public open space amenity grass and this must be recognised and the necessary commitment made. Sites should only be developed for recreation end uses where a need for the facility can be identified.

In restoring a site for recreational use it is important that the quality of restoration is such that the use can be sustained. Adequate slopes, soil depths and textures are essential in providing good drainage conditions.

DLG will not normally provide for a sufficient standard of restoration for good quality playing fields. Grants from other sources such as the Sports Council may be available to provide additional funds.

If sites are restored and maintained to a sufficiently high standard there may be opportunities for income from pitch fees or club rents which should be realised.

9.6.2.6 Mixed End Uses Where sites are restored to mixed end uses it is important that management of the various components is co-ordinated. A number of sites studied showed successful integration of afteruses, the most common combinations being agriculture and woodland, and public open space and woodland.

For larger sites the mixed use strategy can be particularly effective and is to be recommended.

Integration of agriculture with other uses, particularly woodland or public open space, is good policy since the income from the agricultural land may be used to offset the maintenance costs of other land. The integration of agriculture with nature conservation can be particularly beneficial on sites with poor soils where low intensity agricultural use can be used as a management tool.

In restoring sites to mixed end uses, the reclamation scheme should be designed and carried out sensitively. For example areas restored to public open space will not require the same depth of soil as agricultural areas. Soil resources should be concentrated in those areas where they will provide most benefit.

There must be effective liaison between organizations responsible for managing and maintaining the various components of mixed end use sites.

9.6.3 Capital and Maintenance Costs and Performance of Sites

Restoration to nature conservation was found to be a highly cost effective option where low capital and maintenance costs were associated with relatively high levels of benefit (Section 8.3). The 'traditional' public open spaces of mown grass with standard trees, particularly in small urban sites, were costly to reclaim and maintain and performance was relatively low. Larger sites were more cost effective as a result of economies of scale. Reducing mowing frequencies and planting more land with woodland blocks would reduce maintenance costs. Recreation sites typically had high capital costs and maintenance requirements although the latter were frequently not fulfilled resulting in low performance. Restoration to agriculture has the potential of reducing local authorities' maintenance costs to zero.

References

Burt, A. and Bradshaw, A.D. (1986) *Transforming our Waste Land: The Way Forward,* Department of the Environment, London HMSO.

Corder, M. (1986) Naturalistic Techniques and the Urban Local Authority, in *Environmental Economy* (eds. R. Brooker and M. Corder), Kirklees Metropolitan Borough Council.

Department of the Environment (1985) *Reclamation and Re-use of Derelict Land,* DoE. Circular 28/85, London HMSO.

Farm Contractor (1986) Contract Charges *Farm Contractor 129,* September 1986, ACP Publishers Ltd.

The Groundwork Trust (1986) *Making the Most of Greenspace – a guide to the management of vegetation around towns and cities,* Unpublished report to the DoE.

Helliwell, D.R. (1984) *Economics of Woodland Management,* Chichester, Packard Publishing Limited.

H.M. Government (1986) *Agricultural Holdings Act 1986,* London, HMSO.

H.M. Government (1988) *Local Government Act 1988,* London, HMSO.

H.M. Government (1957 & 1984) *Occupiers Liability Acts,* London, HMSO.

Nix, J. (1986) *Farm Management Pocketbook,* 17th Edition (1987), Wye College London.

Nix, J., Hill P. and Williams, N. (1987) *Land and Estate Management,* Chichester, Packard Publishing Limited.

P.S.A. (1987) *Schedule of Rates for Grounds Maintenance 1987,* London HMSO.

Roger Tym and Partners and Land Use Consultants (1987) *Evaluation of Derelict Land Grant Schemes,* Department of the Environment Inner Cities Research Programme, London, HMSO.

The Scottish Agricultural Colleges (1986) *Farm Management Handbook 1986/87,* The Scottish Agricultural Colleges.

Welsh Development Agency (1987) *Working With Nature,* Welsh Development Agency.

Appendix 1

Site Assessment of Derelict Sites

Before selection of an appropriate afteruse and design of a reclamation scheme can be undertaken it is essential that basic information regarding the site and its surroundings is gathered. This will involve a certain amount of research combined with site inspections. The check list which follows is intended as an *aide memoire* for those involved in site assessments. The information gathered should enable informed decisions regarding suitable afteruses for sites to be made. It is important that those involved in site assessment should possess the skills for acquiring the necessary information and a multidisciplinary approach is recommended. A suitable range of expertise would be provided by a team including a planner, engineer, ecologist, landscape architect and land agent.

Once the initial assessment has been made the need for further detailed site investigation work may be indicated. This might include investigations of buried structures, mine shafts, etc., topographical surveys, analysis of soils for contamination or nutrient status, etc. Using the site data the need for reclamation of the site can be assessed, its suitability for the various afteruses and the need for regrading, import of soils etc. determined.

1. History of Site

1.1 Map evidence

1.1.1 What do large scale O.S. plans of site reveal of site history, particularly with regard to location of structures, lagoons, waste tips, mine shafts, etc?

1.1.2 Do other plans of site exist e.g. works plans, in Public Records Office or similar archives?

1.2 Other evidence

1.2.1 Is there any published historical information regarding the site in local histories, directories, etc?

1.2.2 Is there any relevant material in Public Records Office or similar archive?

1.2.3 Do local residents and former employees have any knowledge regarding the history of the site?

2. Land Tenure, Safety, Statutory Undertakers and Services

2.1 Land Tenure

2.1.1 Is land in local authority ownership?

2.1.2 If not, is land in single or multiple ownership?

2.1.3 Is land occupied by owners or tenanted?

2.1.4 Is acquisition feasible?

2.1.5 Are there any tenure or legal restrictions which would impose constraints on the afteruse of the land?

2.2 Safety

2.2.1 Is the site unsafe in its present condition, e.g. open mine shafts, deep water, open culverts, unfenced railway line, etc?

2.2.2 What measures would need to be taken to make the site safe?

2.3 Statutory Undertakers and Services

2.3.1 Do gas pipes, electricity cables, sewerage or water pipes cross the site?

2.3.2 Do any other pipleines cross the site?

2.3.3 Do telephone cables cross the site?

2.3.4 Are there any wells on the site?

3. Physical Characteristics of the Site and its Surroundings

3.1 Land

3.1.1 What are the geological characteristics of the area?

3.1.2 Are underground workings or mine shafts present?

3.1.3 Are there any other indicators of actual or potential surface instability e.g. presence of old lagoons, slumping of slopes, erosion of slopes, etc?

3.1.4 Are soils or soil forming materials suitable for use in restoration present on the site, and if so what quantity?

3.1.5 If soils are present, what is their general physical quality particularly in terms of texture and structure?

3.1.6 What are the topographical characteristics of the site e.g. major slopes, areas of relatively flat land, valleys, etc?

3.1.7 Does the topography of the site impose constraints on the choice of potential afteruse?

3.2 Hydrology

3.2.1 What is the current pattern of surface drainage?

3.2.2 Are springs or issues of groundwater present on site?

3.2.3 Is there open water on site?

3.2.4 Are low lying marshy areas present?

3.2.5 Is there evidence of contamination of any water on site?

3.2.6 Does the hydrology of the site impose constraints on the choice of potential afteruse?

3.3 Climate

3.3.1 Are there any climatic factors (e.g. exposure, rainfall, temperature, etc.) which may impose constraints on the potential afteruses?

4. Ecological Characteristics of the State and its Surroundings

4.1 Vegetation

4.1.1 What proportion of the site has a vegetation cover?

4.1.2 Is the presence or absence of cover associated with particular soils or waste materials?

4.1.3 What are the major vegetation types present e.g. marsh, grassland, woodland etc?

4.1.4 What is the species composition of plant communities within each vegetation type?

4.1.5 Is plant growth vigorous?

4.1.6 Do plants exhibit any symptoms of toxicity or deficiency?

4.1.7 Is the vegetation of conservation interest at a neighbourhood, local, county, regional or national scale?

4.1.8 What do the species present indicate regarding the site in terms of fertility, toxicity, nature of substrates, drainage, stability, etc?

4.1.9 Are any areas of vegetation suitable for retention and incorporation in a restoration scheme?

4.1.10 What is the nature of the vegetation on land surrounding the site?

4.1.11 Is there potential for natural colonization of the site from the surrounding vegetation?

4.2 Other ecological characteristics

4.2.1 To what extent does the topography and vegetation of the site provide a habitat for wildlife, including invertebrates, mammals, birds?

4.2.2 Is the site of wildlife interest at the neighbourhood, local, regional, county or national level?

4.2.3 Is there scope for conserving wildlife as part of a reclamation scheme?

5 Land Use and Landscape

5.1 Land use

5.1.1 Is the land in an urban, urban fringe or rural situation?

5.1.2 What are the current uses of the site itself including both formal and informal uses?

5.1.3 To what extent should existing uses of the site be accommodated in a reclamation scheme?

5.1.4 What are the land uses in the area surrounding the site?

5.1.5 To what extent do the surrounding land uses impose constraints on the choice of afteruse for the site?

5.1.6 Are there likely to be significant future changes in surrounding land uses?

5.1.7 To what extent could the restored site be integrated with other land use in the vicinity?

5.1.8 To what extent does design of site need to be flexible to accommodate possible changes in surrounding land use?

5.2 Landscape

5.2.1 What are the essential landscape characteristics of the surroundings of the site?

5.2.2 What is the scale of the surrounding landscape e.g. intimate, open, extensive, etc?

5.2.3 To what extent does the site itself influence the landscape? Include positive and negative effects.

5.2.4 Are there any trees or buildings on the site worthy of preservation?

5.2.5 What are the landscape considerations which should guide the design of a reclamation scheme?

6. Population and Access

6.1 Population

6.1.1 What is the density of population in the area surrounding the site in general terms?

6.1.2 Is this population likely to increase, decrease or remain stable?

6.2 Access

6.2.1 Is there ready access to the site from the immediate surroundings?

6.2.2 Are there barriers to access such as private land, major roads, railways, rivers, etc?

6.2.3 Is the nature of, size of and access to the site such that its use would be limited to the population of the immediate surroundings or does it have potential for attracting a wider population?

Appendix 2

Further Information
The following are accessible publications which provide practical information relevant to aspects of reclamation and management of derelict land covered by this report.

A2.1 Derelict Land Reclamation Schemes

Department of the Environment (1985) *Reclamation and Re-use of Derelict Land.* Circular 28/85 London, HMSO.

J.U.R.U.E. (1987) *Greening City Sites: Good Practice in Urban Regeneration.* Department of the Environment London, HMSO.

National Audit Office (1988) *Department of the Environment: Derelict Land Grant.* Report by the Comptroller and Auditor General, London, HMSO.

Roger Tym and Partners and Land Use Consultants (1987) *Evaluation of Derelict Land Grant Schemes.* Department of the Environment Inner Cities Research Programme, London, HMSO.

A2.2 Land Reclamation – Problems and Solutions

Bradshaw, A.D. and Chadwick, M.J. (1980) *The Restoration of Land.* Oxford, Blackwell.

Burt, A. and Bradshaw, A.D. (1986) *Transforming our Waste Land: The Way Forward.* Department of the Environment, London, HMSO.

Coppin, N.J. and Bradshaw, A.D. (1982) *Quarry Reclamation.* London, Mining Journal Books.

Dutton, R.A. and Bradshaw, A.D. (1982) *Land Reclamation in Cities.* Department of the Environment, London, HMSO.

Gemmell, R.P. (1977) *Colonization of Industrial Wasteland.* London, Edward Arnold.

A2.3 Contaminated Land Reclamation

Cairney, T. (Ed.) (1987) *Reclaiming Contaminated Land.* Glasgow, Blackie.

Department of the Environment/Welsh Office (1987) *Development of Contaminated Land.* Circular 21/87 (DoE), 22/87 (WO) London, HMSO.

Environmental Resources Ltd. (1988) *Problems arising from the Redevelopment of Gas Works and Similar Sites* (Second Edition). Department of the Environment, London, HMSO.

Interdepartmental Committee on the Redevelopment of Contaminated Land
— Notes on the redevelopment of landfill sites. ICRCL 17/78
— Notes on the development of gas works sites. ICRCL 18/79
— Notes on the redevelopment of sewage works and farms. ICRCL 23/79
— Notes on the redevelopment of scrapyards and similar sites. ICRCL 42/80
— Guidance on the assessment and redevelopment of contaminated land. ICRCL 59/83
— Notes on the fire hazards of contaminated land. ICRCL 61/84
— Asbestos on contaminated sites. ICRCL 64/85

A2.4 Naturalistic Techniques of Vegetation Establishment and Maintenance

Brooker, R. and Corder, M. (Eds.) (1986) *Environmental Economy.* London, E. and F.N. Spon.

Corder, M. and Brooker, R. (1981) *Natural Economy.* Kirklees Metropolitan Borough Council.

Emery, M. (1986) *Promoting Nature in Towns and Cities.* London, Croom Helm.

Welsh Development Agency (1987) *Working With Nature.* Welsh Development Agency.

A2.5 Grassland

Countryside Commission (1980) *Grassland Establishment in Countryside Recreation Areas.* Advisory Series No. 13. Cheltenham, Countryside Commission.

Lowday, J.E. and Wells, T.C.E. (1977) *The Management of Grassland and Heathland in Country Parks.* Report No. CCP105. Cheltenham, Countryside Commission.

National Turfgrass Council (1983) *Grassing of Temporary Vacant Sites Without Importing Topsoil.* Bingley, National Turfgrass Council.

Robinson, S. (Ed.) (1982) *Grassing of Temporary Vacant Sites.* Workshop Report No. 1. Bingley, National Turfgrass Council.

Shildrick, J.P. (Ed.) (1985) *Better Grass, Greater Value.* Proceedings of the 3rd National Turfgrass Conference. Bingley, National Turfgrass Council.

A2.6 Woodland

Brooks, A. (1980) *Woodlands.* Reading, British Trust for Conservation Volunteers.

Davies, R.J. (1987) *Trees and Weeds.* Forestry Commission Handbook 2. London, HMSO.

Evans, J. (1984) *Silviculture of Broadleaved Woodland.* Forestry Commission Bulletin 62, London, HMSO.

Helliwell, D.R. (1984) *Economics of Woodland Management.* Chichester, Packard Publishing.

Hibberd, B.G. (Ed.) (1986) *Forestry Practice*. Forestry Commission Bulletin 14. London, HMSO.

Hibberd, B.G. (Ed.) (1988) *Farm Woodland Practice*. Forestry Commission Handbook 3. London, HMSO.

Hibberd, B.G. (Ed.) (1989) *Urban Forestry Practice*. Forestry Commission Handbook 5. London, HMSO.

Insley, H. (Ed.) (1988) *Farm Woodland Planning*. Forestry Commission Bulletin 80. London, HMSO.

Irving, J.A. (1985) *The Public in Your Woods*. Chichester, Packard Publishing.

Williamson, D.R. and Lane, P.B. (1989) *The Use of Herbicides in the Forest*. 3rd Edition. Forestry Commission. Fieldbook 8. London, HMSO.

Wilson, K. (1985) *A Guide to the Reclamation of Mineral Workings to Forestry*. Research and Development Paper 141, Forestry Commission. Edinburgh.

A2.7 Land Tenure

Muir Watt, J.A. (1987) *Agricultural Holdings*. 13th Edition. London, Sweet and Maxwell.

Scammell and Denison (1989) *The Law of Agricultural Holdings*. 7th Edition (Revised). London, Butterworth.

A2.8 Miscellaneous

Agate, E. (1983) *Footpaths*, Wallingford, British Trust for Conservation Volunteers.

Agate, E. (1986) *Fencing*. Wallingford, British Trust for Conservation Volunteers.

Audit Commission (1988a) *Local Authority Property: A Management Overview*. London, HMSO.

Audit Commission (1988b) *Competitive Management of Parks and Green Spaces*. London, HMSO.

Brooks, A. (1980) *Hedging*. Reading, British Trust for Conservation Volunteers.

Brooks, A. (1981) *Waterways and Wetlands*. Reading, British Trust for Conservation Volunteers.

Joint Council for Landscape Industries (1987) *Grounds Maintenance. Model Form of Tender and Contract Documents*. Keighley, J.C.L.I.

Leay, M.J., Rowe, J. and Young, J.D. (1986) *Management Plans*. Report CCP 206. Cheltenham, Countryside Commission.

Nature Conservancy Council (1988) *Site Management Plans for Nature Conservation*. Peterborough, Nature Conservancy Council.

Nix, J., Hill, P. and Williams, N. (1987) *Land and Estate Management*. Chichester. Packard Publishing.

Printed in the United Kingdom for Her Majesty's Stationery Office
Dd. 292572 C13 2/90 488 12521